Beyond the
Lean Office

A Novel on Progressing
from Lean Tools to
Operational Excellence

Beyond the Lean Office

Kevin J. Duggan

CRC Press
Taylor & Francis Group
Boca Raton   London   New York

CRC Press is an imprint of the
Taylor & Francis Group, an **informa** business

A PRODUCTIVITY PRESS BOOK

CRC Press
Taylor & Francis Group
6000 Broken Sound Parkway NW, Suite 300
Boca Raton, FL 33487-2742

Printed on acid-free paper
Version Date: 20160229

International Standard Book Number-13: 978-1-4987-1248-4 (Paperback)

Library of Congress Cataloging-in-Publication Data

Names: Duggan, Kevin J., author.
Title: Beyond the lean office : a novel on progressing from lean tools to
operational excellence / Kevin J. Duggan.
Description: Boca Raton, FL : CRC Press, 2015. | Includes bibliographical
references and index.
Identifiers: LCCN 2016001670 | ISBN 9781498712484 (alk. paper)
Subjects: LCSH: Organizational effectiveness. | Organizational behavior. |
Organizational change.
Classification: LCC HD58.9 .D837 2015 | DDC 658.4/013--dc23
LC record available at http://lccn.loc.gov/2016001670

Visit the Taylor & Francis Web site at
http://www.taylorandfrancis.com

and the CRC Press Web site at
http://www.crcpress.com

Contents

Preface

Operational Excellence. Corporate leaders embrace it for a competitive edge in today's challenging global market. It is heralded as the antidote to slipping revenues. And industry titans like Toyota tout it as a business necessity (Liker 2004). But what exactly is it?

While more and more companies are aggressively pursuing Operational Excellence by employing Six Sigma, Lean, and other continuous improvement methods, the concept itself remains vague. It has yet to be practically defined in a way that can be taught and applied, especially to industries other than manufacturing. The result: companies comprising mostly offices and business processes, such as insurers, hospital administrative practices, financial companies, banks, and service organizations lack an applicable definition of Operational Excellence. And there is little (if any) written material on how to achieve it in the office—until now.

To achieve Operational Excellence, it takes more than just a strong leader with passion and drive. The key ingredient is practical knowledge that can be applied quickly and easily by following a process, a step-by-step guide to move the office services from point A to point B. The practical knowledge and the guide together create a road map that can be read and shared with each employee to rapidly move a company forward.

That process is described in the pages that follow. The knowledge is practical and hands on, but told through a story to make it more applicable to what companies face each day. It is not intended to solve problems in the office or provide solutions. In fact, this type of thinking is what often restricts companies from achieving Operational Excellence. Rather, the information provided explores different concepts and ways of thinking to offer a fresh look at the office and business processes. It is intended to educate and teach companies *how to grow their businesses by achieving Operational Excellence in their offices.*

Once applied to all areas of the organization, the end result is a business that does not require management intervention to deliver the services provided by the office. Instead, management focuses on offense, or activities that grow the business. The net result is *a business that is designed to grow year after year.*

Enjoy reading, apply the knowledge, and grow your business.

REFERENCE

Liker, Jeffery K. *The Toyota Way: 14 Management Principles from the World's Greatest Manufacturer.* New York: McGraw-Hill, 2004.

Kevin J. Duggan

Founder, Institute for Operational Excellence
President, Duggan Associates

Acknowledgments

While many people at the Institute for Operational Excellence contributed their time and efforts to developing the concepts and writing for this book, the project team spent many long hours creating and refining this material. The Institute would like to recognize and thank James Marrese and Kirk Bolton for making this book possible.

Many other people supported the project team in their endeavors. The Institute would like to recognize and thank Elizabeth Duggan and Jennifer Krider for their hard work and tireless dedication.

Author

Kevin J. Duggan has more than 30 years' experience applying advanced Lean techniques to achieve Operational Excellence and is the author of three books on the subject: *Design for Operational Excellence: A Breakthrough Strategy for Business Growth* (McGraw-Hill, 2011); *Creating Mixed Model Value Streams* (Productivity Press, 2002); and *The Office That Grows Your Business: Achieving Operational Excellence in Your Business Processes* (The Institute for Operational Excellence, 2009). A recognized authority on Operational Excellence, Kevin has contributed to publications such as *Industry Week, Aviation Week, Food Engineering, Flow Control, Assembly, Lean Management Journal*, and *Plant Services* and has appeared on CNN and the Fox Business Network. He is a frequent keynote speaker, master of ceremonies, and panelist at both public and private conferences globally and lectures graduate students in colleges throughout the United States.

In 1998, Kevin founded Duggan Associates, an international training and advisory firm that assists companies in applying advanced Lean techniques to their manufacturing and office operations through hands-on support and workshops on topics such as creating mixed model value streams, creating flow through shared resources, creating flow through the supply chain, creating business process value streams, and Lean product development. Since Duggan Associates' inception, Kevin has helped entities from Fortune 50 corporations to small businesses with single-site operations in just about every industry, including insurance, engineering development, financial services, aerospace, energy, and manufacturing, such as United Technologies Corporation, FMC Technologies, Caterpillar, Pratt & Whitney, Singapore Airlines, IDEX Corporation, GKN, and Parker Hannifin. In 2007, Kevin founded the Institute for Operational Excellence, the leading educational center on Operational Excellence, which provides resources such as workshops, online training, how-to articles, and books to a global community of members.

1

Prologue

I remember the day that changed my professional life forever: the day I learned things that altered my view of continuous improvement; the day I saw a business that had harnessed its efforts not only to get better each day but also to improve business growth and performance; the day I learned that a company that achieves Operational Excellence is much more than an organization that eliminates waste and does things efficiently—it is a company that has developed and applied fundamental principles for sustained business growth.

It was quite a day.

On that day, I heard Operational Excellence defined in a way that was easy to understand, applicable to all levels of an organization, and effective at aligning everyone not toward a vision, but toward a destination. I also had the privilege of seeing the definition come to life when I walked through an office and saw Operational Excellence in action.

Don't get me wrong—I am not a newcomer to all of this. I was previously well read in continuous improvement and was striving to create a culture of continuous improvement at my company. I specialized in business processes and improving office functions. I had used my knowledge of Lean, Six Sigma, and the successful Toyota Production System to make improvements in my company's business processes recently and thought I knew how to effectively use the latest tools and techniques.

But, I was wrong. Sure, the tools worked, and by applying them, I was making progress. The journey seemed endless, though, week after week finding areas to improve and applying tools, with no destination in sight. I realized on that fateful day that anything we do to try to improve our business processes in the office must be geared toward supporting business growth. It not only has to drive bottom-line results; it has to lay a foundation from which we can grow our business.

As if that was not enough of a game changer, I was shocked to learn that companies achieve Operational Excellence *in months*, not years. And, it does not require a strong leader to drive the change and sustain it. It takes education, and boy did I get some. I discovered that Operational Excellence is not a vague or ambiguous place but rather a tangible destination that can be achieved by following a road map. Most important, because Operational Excellence is achieved through a process, it can be taught, which means the knowledge can be shared and applied quickly throughout the entire organization.

Even though I did not get all the details when I learned about Operational Excellence for the first time, the knowledge was simple and intuitive. I understood enough to be able to go back and begin educating people in my own office, including my boss, about the concepts. To think there was a time when I had never heard of takt capability, workflow cycles, guaranteed turnaround times, single-point initialization, standard work at the flow level, and *an office that operates without management...*

But, I am getting ahead of myself. The real story begins a few days earlier, when I returned from a weeklong conference. While I was gone, something had gone seriously wrong at my office.

2

The Hornet's Nest

It was Monday morning, but I was anxious to get to work after a week at a conference full of insurance adjusters, most of them excited about recent changes to the Medicare/Medicaid verbiage. It is a topic we have to untangle for our business plans, but I was admittedly distant, more curious to see how my team in the office was doing in my absence. The last few weeks had been hectic, but everyone seemed to pull together with some creative solutions. I had left the office confident in how my team would perform while I was away. Confirming my expectations, I did not receive any calls during the conference—a good, albeit unusual, sign.

At the conference registration, I bumped into Peyton Peterson, a classmate from my undergraduate days. I had lost track of Peyton over the years, but at these massive conferences, I had learned the hard way that it is generally best to share a table with someone you know versus a stranger who may have peculiar habits. Recalling Peyton's studious characteristics and common sense, I asked to share a table.

Peyton's reply surprised me: "Sure, maybe we can catch up on things during break. But I really want to learn this material."

Good choice, Pat, I thought to myself. "No distractions here," I said.

Over the course of the week, I learned that Peyton faced the same career dilemma I had a year earlier, so I offered some counsel—at breaks, of course. I explained to Peyton that I had been working in the accounts receivable department at a local 500-bed hospital. "The job was secure, the hospital was solvent, and I had moved up from a college intern spot to a full-time position. I had overcome my earlier identity as an intern and convinced management that I was ready for a supervisory role."

"How did you accomplish that?" asked Peyton. "I'm still suffering a bit from the intern image and would like to understand what you did to get them to recognize your abilities. My goal is to become the divisional expert on this Medicare/Medicaid topic we're learning about this week."

"Some of it was luck," I said. "But mostly it was lemonade from lemons. Over a few years, I had made numerous lateral moves that exposed me to many areas of the business and several departmental managers. I observed and analyzed different management styles and chose to emulate those that worked best as I worked on my own future. I felt pretty fortunate to have had those opportunities, not to mention all the technical knowledge I gained from bouncing around between different areas of the business."

"I see how the lemonade strategy worked for you," said Peyton. "But I'm on my second manager now, studying Lean tools, and I don't exactly get the feeling that I'm on the fast track. I think it's going to take something else."

"I was lucky … sort of," I explained. "My employees performed well, met and exceeded the goals set for them, and made me a valuable asset to the company in the process. I thought that was going to be my ticket to bigger and better things, but I soon learned that being a valued supervisor wasn't necessarily the best thing for my career. It was clear that I had become so good at what I was doing that I was never going to get promoted.

"Maybe I should have discussed my situation with my manager or someone who could have given me advice. But, as they say, timing is everything. I took a phone call from a recruiter and entertained an inquiry from an insurance company. Even though I didn't know anything about claims processing, I was a lifetime learner and a good supervisor, and knew I was ready to get my feet wet as a department manager."

"So, you didn't get into management by becoming a technical expert?" asked Peyton.

"Well, yes and no," I said. "Initially, I became technically savvy to demonstrate competence to my superiors. Then, I started looking at the bigger picture and where I wanted to be in 3 to 5 years. The fastest way to get somewhere is to know where your journey will take you. Keep that in mind as you strive for that expert status you mentioned. You might be valuable, but you might be *too* valuable to be promoted."

I wondered if I was still trying to justify my decision to leave the hospital. Things had been comfortable there, and steady. Insurance, on the other hand, is about risk, in more ways than one, and the past 8 months at my new job had not always been comfortable.

The insurance claims business was new to me when I started. In my prior experience in hospital accounts receivable, I had dealt with the insurance market for years and learned that some claims processors were much more capable than others. My reputation was equally known. One of the less respected but larger insurance companies had gotten to know me better than either of us would have liked because of constant expedites, quality problems, and settlement errors. They had some chronic issues they genuinely wanted to fix, but they continued to be unsuccessful. When the recruiter contacted me, she explained the situation, their challenges, and their commitment to fixing this problem by hiring a professional from the outside.

I was initially intrigued, but she really got my attention when she told me they wanted to hire a manager who could apply Lean teachings. It was an exciting challenge to start fresh at a company and have the chance to fix some of their problems.

A cheery voice from the ordering window at my local coffeehouse interrupted my reflections.

"Good morning, Pat. Your usual?"

"Yes, grande latte, two shots of espresso, thanks."

Moments later, I took my coffee and drove toward the office, sipping while trying to avoid the potholes and the few other drivers on the road.

When I got to work, I easily found a good parking spot in the lot, grabbed my briefcase, and cradled that precious coffee as I stepped out of my car. Soon, I was walking briskly toward the seven-story building and planning my day in my head. I had come in early to try to make a dent in the backlog that was sure to have accumulated while I was at the conference. At this hour, there would be no people, and no people meant no distractions.

When I was almost within the shadow of the building, it happened. The lights came on in my boss's corner office on the third floor.

It is OK, I thought. I will just quietly enter my office. I can still get an hour to myself to wade through all the e-mails, voice mails, and memos that are no doubt waiting for me. After that, when the workday officially starts, I will have finished my coffee and can check in with Chris in the corner office.

I can take the stairs rather than the elevator. It will be a bit more clumsy with this coffee, but I can control the staircase door and close it quietly to get in unnoticed. There is no need to disturb the boss, who probably wants to get on top of the chaos before a fresh round hits this week. This way, we will both be able to get a good, uninterrupted start.

I made it through the lobby, up the staircases, and into my office without any loud noises: no doors slamming, no laptops crashing onto desks, no chairs banging into walls. Generally, Chris sings out a greeting when it becomes apparent I have arrived, and the absence of a welcome suggested I might have some solitude.

I carefully set the coffee on my desk and started to organize the mess, a healthy dose of voice mails, e-mails, and Post-it® notes. Where to begin? Post-it notes are urgent because they were delivered in person. Voice mail is next because someone could not wait for a conventional response. E-mail is next, then the in-basket.

I pulled the Post-it notes off my desk like I was an archeologist doing a forensic analysis at a dig site. Obviously, the ones on top were the most recent, but perhaps they had a linkage to some of the ones buried deeper. I reviewed them one by one, matched them with their predecessors, and then arranged the piles into two groups: action items and status reports. There was only one action item, and that could wait until everyone else arrived.

Next was voice mail. I reached for the phone and it rang right when I touched the handset, causing me to nearly spill my coffee all over my desk. I caught my breath and grabbed the receiver before the second ring, thinking I might be able to prolong my solitude if Chris had not heard it: Answer it quietly.

"Good morning, this is Pat O'Malley," I said in a strong but quiet tone, realizing then that I had not had the presence of mind to check the caller ID before picking up. "How can I help you?"

"Aha! I sensed you were here, and I saw your office light spilling into the hallway," said Chris. "But I expected you to stop by as usual. Have you checked your e-mail yet?"

"No," I replied. "I was just getting to my voice mail when you called. What can I do for you?"

"So you haven't gotten to your e-mail yet?" Chris repeated. "Then you don't know that Mercy Hospital, one of our biggest customers, is irate? I'm surprised no one contacted you while you were gone. Well, I'm glad you're here early. Come to my office. You don't need to go through all the e-mail strings now; I'll fill you in on what's important. But you'll probably want to read through everything later tonight."

Later tonight? What did that mean? What had happened?

During my 8 months here, Chris had never been that direct. Whatever this was about, it must be serious—and might signal the end of the new-associate honeymoon. I grabbed my notepad and hurried into Chris's office.

"What's the situation?" I asked.

"Last week, we let a very important claim drop through the cracks, and it was late getting out to Mercy Hospital, one of our biggest customers. We were missing simple information on the claim; it got sidelined, and we didn't even notice it was late. Wednesday morning, the day it was targeted to clear, Mercy called us to get the status. When we had to request the missing information, it was obvious that we were just starting the claim. Worse, they said they'd charted a downward trend in our performance. They actually *anticipated* the claim would be late based on the poor performance record we'd generated over the past quarter, and since this claim was particularly large, they'd put us on watch.

"I had to get involved and was told by your team that for the past 8 weeks, they'd been limiting the number of expedited claims allowed at any time to two, and they had already hit their max when the Mercy one rolled around. They were quick to explain that this system was effective in eliminating the daily peaks and valleys in their workload and had allowed them to be more productive with fewer priority shifts."

At least my team understood the new system, could explain it, and were disciplined to the point of defending it. But, what had gone wrong? We had all agreed to the changes during a kaizen, or rapid improvement event. We tested the rules for 6 weeks, made adjustments as needed, and had a challenge to the "two-per-day" limit during the whole trial period.

I wanted to speak, but Chris was not even taking a breath.

"I then persuaded, no, I *told* them to expedite the Mercy Hospital claim, and Bob said he would shepherd it through. This was last Wednesday."

We did not count on a claim being sidelined that long, but what am I supposed to do? Change our standard operating procedure to make sure we always take care of Mercy Hospital first? Our intention was to treat all expedited claims the same, regardless of the customer, and Chris knew this. We had spoken about the issue at length when the system first rolled out.

"What's the status now?" I asked. "Did we get the check cut on Wednesday?"

"It finished on Friday at noon, 2 days later than they expected it," said Chris. "Your team offered reasons why it took so long, but I know this process. I worked my way up by performing every task, and it shouldn't have taken that long to expedite—expedite!—a claim. There's no reasonable explanation for why we missed the target, just excuses! You know time is money, especially in this economy, and we cost Mercy 2 extra days.

"But that's not even the real issue. What's more concerning is that one of our customers seemed to know more about our performance than we did. So, I had the Information Technology Department create a report for the last quarter showing how long each claim took to process, plus actual versus planned completion dates. I confirmed the downward trend, not only for Mercy Hospital, but also for most of the claims we process. It creates a hefty cash float, which is positive for us but bad for our customers. Based on our performance over the last quarter and what Mercy Hospital told me, we could be in danger of driving them to another partner. And, for all we know, other customers are thinking the same thing and just not telling us. Do you realize the financial hit we would take if that happened?"

Yes, I did. That was one of the things I came to fix.

"Pat, I could ask you a number of questions right now, but I don't think you'd have answers for any of them. I realize you didn't gain your experience processing claims here like I did, but that doesn't matter now. We need results, and we need to come up with a corrective action plan very soon that demonstrates how committed we are to improving our performance for all of our customers. We can't just create a Mercy Hospital group and use it to expedite their claims. That won't get to the heart of the issue. We need to get better for everyone, or we'll lose them all.

"The corrective action plan is your department's responsibility. I want to have that plan in my hands for review Tuesday afternoon, one that applies to Mercy Hospital *and* every other customer."

Chris paused for a second, then leaned in to give me some more personal guidance.

"Look, you've only been here for 8 months, and already I've seen some improvements. But we, and you, have a lot riding on this. I'm really troubled about the expedite criteria and the limit your team told me about. How can we serve our customers when we're only allowed to process two expedited claims at any given time? You can't control when something has to be expedited, Pat, you have to react to it. That's what good managers do: react, adjust, direct as needed, and get everyone together in a meeting to fix the problem. I don't think you can limit the number of expedited claims, so that's where I'd start to look."

"OK, Chris, I won't let you down," I said. "Things have been getting better over the past 2 months, at least from where I sit. I understand business, so I recognize our customers' cash flow is important. I'll start pulling some strategy together now and gather the team when they get in. I'll get right on this, and I'll check in with you later today to let you know where I'm headed."

"OK," said Chris. "But remember, it isn't just me you have to satisfy; it's our entire customer base. We can't lose Mercy Hospital, or any other account, for that matter. We brought you in here 8 months ago to fix things, and much of our reasoning was based on how relentless you were in managing our account. I expect your doggedness to continue now. I know most of the associates in your department have other duties besides claims processing. They always have and always will. But, this tardiness can't continue. Let me know if … ."

"I'm on it."

FROM THE AUTHOR

Traditional Lean teaches us to eliminate waste by looking at areas where non-value-added activities occur, then use tools such as kaizens to reduce or eliminate the non-value-added activities. This approach has been successful in the areas addressed. During kaizen events, management's role is to identify improvement objectives, set goals and targets, provide leadership, and remove barriers that might prevent the team from accomplishing its goals. Management generally avoids prescribing or dictating specific solutions to the team, as frontline ownership of the improvement initiative is critical to its long-term success. Creating team-level ownership ingrains the improvement into the culture and solidifies the new way of doing things—until something goes wrong.

As soon as something goes wrong, the typical response is for managers to step in, provide direction, override the existing way of doing things, and fix the problem to get everything back on track, usually by holding meetings and telling everyone what to do—the exact opposite of the approach used during the kaizen. We can think of this as "management muscle." Leadership reinserts itself into the operation to fix the problem and "muscle the work" through to the customer, regardless of the system currently in use. This frequently involves holding many meetings to set direction, developing a corrective action plan, and then monitoring and following up on what was done to ensure the problem stays fixed. In fact, many managers spend a good deal of time each day doing this and taking care of other issues as they arise.

When we rely on management muscle to fix problems, it becomes established as protocol, and the office ends up depending on this response indefinitely. This not only undermines the work of previous improvement efforts but also limits management's ability to work on other things, to the detriment of the business as a whole. While the original improvement initiative likely eliminated waste and improved performance, management still finds it necessary to step in and correct things when they go wrong.

3

The Investigation

My mind was racing as I stepped out of Chris's office. I need to get my team together, go over what happened, get everyone on the same page, and then talk to them about the problems they were having with the new improvements we implemented. Once I do that, I'll come up with some solutions that apply to our major customers, sell the plan to Chris, and then begin implementing it immediately.

I heard the elevator doors open on my floor, but Bob was the only one who got off, and I quickly approached him in the elevator alcove. I wanted to learn the details Chris did not know. Bob had been with the business for years and knew all the processes. He had become the answer man for everything but, unlike me, seemed to be content with his status and had no desire to get into management.

"Bob, I'm glad you're here early," I said as he got off the elevator. "Chris informed me that Mercy Hospital is really upset. I need to know what went wrong."

Bob stared at me dumbfounded, a glazed look coming over his eyes like he had told this same story many times before. "So, Chris told you what happened?"

"Well, I was briefed on the high points and told to develop a corrective action plan, but I really don't know the details. Can you fill me in?"

"Sure," he said, regaining some of his composure. "I figured you'd be here now, so I came in early, too. The Mercy Hospital claim started on time but was missing some information. It was sidelined so we could obtain the info, but when the hospital called to inquire about the delivery, no one could find the file. After turning the department upside down, we eventually found it, still incomplete, so then we had to expedite the claim, even though it didn't fit our criteria and we had already reached our limit for the day. We got it out on Friday at noon.

"I didn't bother calling you because when Chris said, 'Bob, expedite this claim, *now*, and I don't care about the criteria,' it was pretty clear what I needed to do. At that point, it was just a matter of doing it. Whether you knew or not wouldn't have changed things, so I decided to leave you alone at the conference."

"OK, thanks for filling me in," I said. "As for Mercy, I'm not sure what to do right now. But the bigger issue is figuring out how to reverse the downward trend in timeliness, not just for Mercy, but for all our accounts."

I wondered what I would have done if I had been around when everything happened. Would I have overridden the procedures? Would that have even been the right answer? Or, would it have just opened the floodgates to more in the future? I collected myself and turned my attention back to Bob.

"Here's what we're going to do. I want to get the team together and review how a claim is processed. I know it, and you know it, but I'm not sure everyone else understands what happens. Get everyone in the conference room when they come in and we'll go through the steps. Then, I want to hear all the problems they're having so I can figure out a solution."

Bob turned and hurried away as I began to gather my thoughts. I only had a few minutes to frame the objective, scope, and strategy for the meeting. I decided to review the departmental organizational chart, make copies, and bring them with me so everyone could see where everyone else fits in (Figure 3.1).

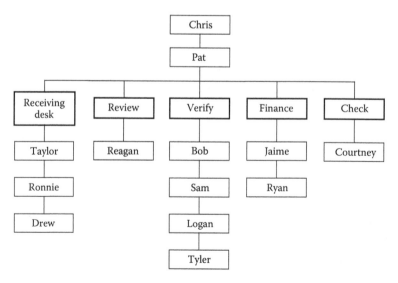

FIGURE 3.1
The departmental organizational chart.

I assembled my materials in the conference room and waited for people to arrive. "Good morning," I said, as everyone made their way into the room and situated themselves. "I'm sure you all know we had a problem with the Mercy Hospital claim last week, and I heard from Chris that our track record for timeliness is trending downward. We're on the bubble now, at risk of losing customers, and we need to examine our procedures to improve our delivery reliability, fast."

With the objective stated, it was time to nail down the scope.

"As if that wasn't enough, Chris has tasked us with improving claims processing for *all* our customers. Whatever changes we make must be global so they impact everyone, not just Mercy Hospital and our other major accounts. I'm not sure we can do all of that, so we're going to focus first on fixing our big customers. I'm hoping that'll satisfy Chris."

I almost couldn't believe I said that last part out loud.

"Once we square them away, we'll investigate what it'll take to incorporate all our other clients, too. Any questions?"

I intended to pause for an appropriate amount of time and then continue, but Taylor spoke up. "I'm not sure what more we can do for even a *few* of our customers, let alone the major ones, or all of them. We already made improvements to the system months ago. What more does Chris want?"

"I don't know yet," I admitted. "But I know we have to find a way. We can't afford to start losing clients. We've made some good improvements recently, but we need to see what else we can do."

Scope done, strategy was next in line.

"Here's what I want to do," I said, addressing the entire group. "I want to review the steps a claim goes through in our entire department and what happens along the way. If we're going to fix anything, then each person needs to know how they fit into the bigger picture. So, I want you all to briefly explain the activities involved at your step. Nothing too detailed, just a quick overview. Once that's done, I want you to talk to me about the problems you're having, then I'll develop a plan to present to Chris tomorrow."

I distributed the copies of the departmental organizational chart I had brought with me and gave everyone time to look at it.

"All right, are there any questions?" I asked. "None? OK, then what's the first step in processing a claim?"

I added that it might be the Receiving desk and drew an oval on a flip chart with that title (Figure 3.2).

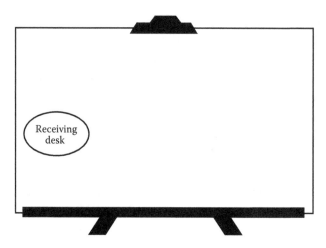

FIGURE 3.2
The Receiving desk, the first process.

"Yes, we get it first," said Taylor. "Me, Ronnie, or Drew, that is. A claim starts here when we receive it from the customer. That could be from a hospital, like Mercy, or from clinics, pharmacies, private practices, nursing homes, or even individual patients. As we all know, the information is usually incomplete, so we often have to contact the customer. Typically, they're hard to reach, and they generally don't understand what information we need or are reluctant to talk to us. Sometimes, our terms are too technical or they're worried they might be getting scammed. It can take a while to get everything we need, but once we have it, we put our packet together for Reagan at Review."

"Thanks, Taylor," I said, jotting down some notes. "Ronnie, Drew, anything to add?" They both shook their heads.

"OK, where do claims go once they're released from Receiving?"

"They go to me over at Review," said Reagan.

I drew a second oval, lower and to the right, and wrote "Review" in it (Figure 3.3).

"I get the packet from the folks at the Receiving desk and then make sure the policy is valid by plugging the information into the system to confirm it's still active, enforced, and up to date. If information is missing or incomplete, I have to give the packet back to Receiving so they can take care of it. But, if the packet has already gone back and forth between us a few times, I might just send it on its way."

"OK," I said, making some mental notes this time. "Where do packets go after that?"

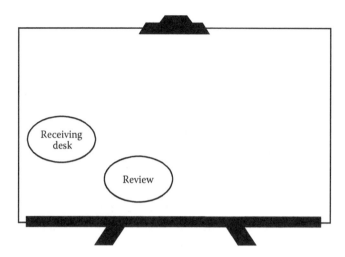

FIGURE 3.3
Review, the second process.

"They go to Verify," said Bob. "Sam, Logan, Tyler, or I handle them."

I drew another oval to the right of Review and labeled it "Verify" (Figure 3.4).

"Essentially, we have to make sure a claim falls within the scope of the policy, so we compare the two. Then, we interpret the claim—who was involved, what was done, when, where, by whom, and so on—to see what's covered. There's a lot of ambiguity in what we see, and sometimes we have to acquire more information or double-check what's there, which only

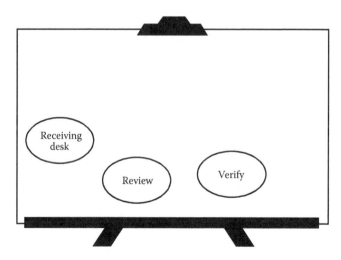

FIGURE 3.4
Verify, the third process.

further delays things. And, of course, we have to document everything we do in case a claim is challenged after we're done with it."

"Thanks, Bob," I said. "What's next?"

"Ryan and I pick it up from there in Finance," said Jaime.

I drew an oval above and to the right of Verify and wrote "Finance" in it (Figure 3.5).

"Once we get everything from Verify, we have to enter some numbers manually into the system, which then calculates the payment. Anything that's considered a large payment is manually double-checked before it's made."

"Thanks, Jaime," I said. "And last but not least, we have Check."

I drew the final oval above and to the left of Finance and then an arrow to indicate the direction in which claims travel (Figure 3.6).

"Yup, that's me," said Courtney from the back of the room. "I enter the information into the system and then the checks are printed, stuffed, stamped, and mailed without me or anyone else ever touching them. That's the end of the process. The claim is complete at this point."

"OK, thanks Courtney," I said. "Now that everyone knows what everyone else does, I want you all to talk to me about any problems you've been having. Don't hold back. Tell me anything that causes you pain during the course of a normal day, including why you think Mercy Hospital got delayed and why you think our trend in timeliness is heading south. I'm going to write your thoughts on the whiteboard and then use them to create a plan to fix all this. Any questions?"

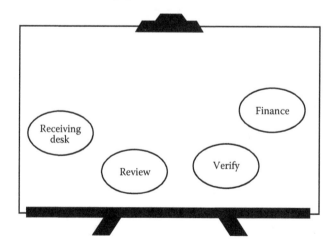

FIGURE 3.5
Finance, the fourth process.

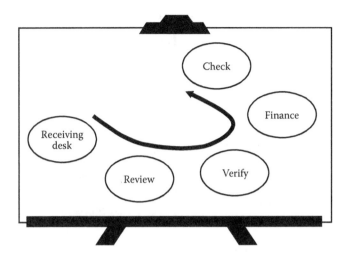

FIGURE 3.6
Check, the fifth and final process. Starting at the Receiving desk, work flows counter-clockwise from process to process.

Everyone looked at one another, but no one offered anything, so I jumped in. "Then, let's start with Taylor, Ronnie, and Drew at Receiving. Talk to me about your problems, what happened with Mercy Hospital, and more generally, why you think we might be trending late."

I went around the room to each department and wrote down their thoughts on the whiteboard. It took most of the morning and early afternoon, but once everyone had said their piece, I thanked them, adjourned the meeting, and then contemplated the list we had created. Based on my knowledge of each department and the additional information they had given me, I added each department's current practice to the list (Figure 3.7).

Where do I start? I thought. I need to come up with a plan I can present to Chris, one that will be satisfying, convincing, and deal with our major customers. Even though Chris wants to involve all our customers, I want to make progress on this, and I think including every customer will be like trying to boil the ocean. So, I'm going to focus on our major customers, including Mercy Hospital, and hope that will be enough for now.

It was getting late, so I grabbed some leftovers from the cafeteria downstairs and brought them back to the conference room so I could continue working. While I ate, I reviewed the departmental issues from the meeting. There were a lot of them, and any number of them might be causing us to miss our promise dates. There also seemed to be lots of commonality and overlap between some of the departments.

Receiving desk issues	Verify issues
• Incomplete information • Illegible information • Too much information, which requires additional sorting and filtering to get at the information that's needed • Communication issues – language barriers to due technical terminology specific to our claims processing procedures • Unpredictable changes in priorities • No assigned maintenance of community equipment – fax paper, printer cartridges, toner, and speed dial numbers not regularly maintained by anyone • **Current Receiving desk department practice** Selective claims processing. Doing the easy ones first, or the ones with the most complete information, and saving the harder ones for later	• Incomplete information • Delays of one day up to one week waiting for information or clarification from the claim submitter, which could be a doctor, patient, hospital, etc. • Subjective approvals, decisions, and interpretations of claims • Changes in priorities • Communication issues – customers lack trust because they are suspicious of scams. They require us to validate our identity • Communication issues – language barriers due to technical terminology specific to our claims processing procedures • **Current Verify department practice** – Double check information before starting to process a claim, and obtain missing information as needed from the claim submitter
Review issues • Subjective approvals, decisions, and interpretations of claims • Incomplete information, which causes returns to the receiving department • Delays of one day up to one week because of incomplete information • Daily changes in what to work on next • **Current Review department practice** – Send ambiguous or incomplete claims back to Receiving, or, sometimes send them to Verify if they've already bounced back and forth a lot	**Finance issues** • No existing standard for system maintenance • Frequent priority changes procedures for paper products and scrapped or voided • **Current Finance department practice** – Manually checks validate and double check large payments
	Check issues • Unscheduled maintenance of equipment and supplies • **Current Check department practice** – Follow security

FIGURE 3.7

The issues described by each department, as well as each department's current practice.

Finishing my food, I decided to try to group the issues by their similarities on a flip chart, figuring this might help shorten the list into something more manageable (Figure 3.8). The chart looked good. It hit the highlights and got to the heart of the matter, concisely identifying what was causing us pain. It certainly seemed like these were the main culprits for our downward trend in timeliness. I felt a degree of control return to my efforts, and I smiled for the first time that day, finally feeling like I was getting somewhere.

It was near quitting time, but before I left, I wanted to update Chris on my investigation. Even though I did not have too much to report at

Possible reasons why we are trending late

(condensed from morning meeting)

1. Frequent reprioritization.

2. Claims forwarded to the next operation with incomplete, erroneous, or illegible information.

3. Too much information, which requires additional levels of filtering to get to the information that's needed.

4. Lack of communication with customers due to their lack of understanding of technical terminology and/or suspicions of our motivations because of scams.

5. Delays in common area equipment servicing.

FIGURE 3.8

A consolidated list of potential causes for lateness.

this point, I felt my narrowed list of possible reasons would demonstrate that I had made some headway and was zeroing in on a solution, which I intended to find tomorrow.

I gathered my things, tore the page off of the flip chart, and headed to Chris's office. I knocked on the door, stood in the threshold, and said, "Hey, Chris, I'd like to update you on what's been going on since we met this morning. Got a minute?"

"Sure, Pat," came the response. "Come on in. I'll feel better knowing what's happened today."

"OK, here's a list of my findings," I said, handing over the page from the flip chart.

Chris reviewed it for about 30 seconds before saying, "So, it all boils down to this? These are the reasons you came up with for the downward trend in timeliness?"

"Yes, I believe so," I said. "I plan to think about it a bit more this evening, but what you have in your hand is a summary of the problems the associates are experiencing. I'm sure if we get rid of most of them, productivity will increase, and the downward trend will be reversed. It'll be tough, and we may have to phase in the changes over time, but that's what I'm going to figure out tomorrow. Then, I'll develop an implementation plan and present it to you at about 1 o'clock tomorrow afternoon, if that's acceptable."

Chris pondered what I'd said, started to speak, stopped, gazed at my list of reasons again, and then replied, "I'll be interested to see that implementation plan, Pat. I don't see a lot of difference between your list here and what I experienced years ago. Some of these issues will be difficult to correct because they involve outside sources like customers, patients, doctors, and so on. However, I agree that if each department eliminates their problems, you might see an upward trend."

Nothing new here? I thought. Is that what I just heard? These problems have not changed over the years? Then, what was done to reverse a downward trend in years past?

"Thanks for the encouragement, I think," I said and faked a smile as I made for the door.

"Oh, and 1 o'clock tomorrow is a problem," said Chris. "I have a meeting that will last until 1:30, so let's start then."

"That's fine," I replied, grateful for the extra 30 minutes to prepare. "See you tomorrow." I made my way out of Chris's office and left for the day.

When I got home, I set my alarm for earlier than normal and fell into bed. I wanted to get an early start tomorrow so I could make as much headway as possible before the meeting. I do not recall falling asleep, but the next morning, I do not recall feeling refreshed either.

FROM THE AUTHOR

Holding meetings to solve problems is deeply embedded in modern office culture, so much so that we often take it for granted when approaching new problems or issues in need of resolution. To help solve problems and create additional insight into their overall scope, we sometimes create process flow diagrams or perhaps even value stream maps to visualize the progression of information and work as they move around the office from activity to activity. Doing this helps everyone to see, understand, and agree on the way work is processed, and this visualization activity is typically illuminating to those involved. Often, it even generates improvement ideas beyond the scope of the problem currently being considered, as employees achieve a better understanding of how their work and tasks have an impact on everyone else and vice versa.

Once the process flow diagram or value stream map has been completed and refined, traditional Lean identifies problems and waste and then targets them for mitigation or (preferably) outright elimination using a variety of tools and techniques, such as root cause analysis, fishbone diagrams, and so on. Utilizing these Lean tools and techniques is intended to improve the performance of the office by making the way it functions less wasteful.

While this approach *can* solve issues and create some limited gains, it is still a function of management muscle. In fact, it supports embedding management into the operation of the office to constantly monitor and solve issues. Once management has stepped in enough times to override the existing way of doing things, management can all too easily *become* the way of doing things all the time.

This approach precludes the creation of any overall end-to-end *design* for how work will move through the office. While there are usually set procedures for how work will be completed at individual activities, there is often no end-to-end design for how information will *proceed* from activity to activity and thus no overall timing for the completion of work from inquiry to delivery of the service to the customer.

This lack of a design creates a continuing opportunity for management to step in when things go wrong. Managers must check to see if work is being completed on time at each step in the office and set priorities, come up with solutions, and give direction when something goes wrong.

Afterward, once the problem has been fixed, the system sometimes is capable of returning to its original way of working without heavy management intervention. However, because there is no set design up front for how work will be completed from start to finish, the more management intervenes over time, the more self-perpetuating its intervention becomes, and the more reliant the office becomes on management for its day-to-day functioning, not just when things go wrong. In this way, the lack of an up-front design for how work will move through the office strongly contributes to heavy management intervention and can be challenging to eliminate.

The key here is what we mean by *design*. By design, we do not mean management getting together and deciding how things should work. The design of information flow in the office must address certain guidelines to create robust information flow. These guidelines are discussed in more detail in the chapters that follow.

4

The Game Plan

I arrived at the office early Tuesday morning, got myself situated, and thought about the list that I created yesterday. I needed to come up with solutions to all five problems on this list, and it was not going to be easy.

I started making notes for corrections and counteractions for each problem. After spending most of the morning sifting through everything, I had developed a plan I felt comfortable presenting to Chris later in the day.

THE PLAN

The following is the plan I developed that day:

1. **Problem: Frequent reprioritization.**

   Solution: We are going to continue with the current expedite policy, but we'll ensure that our major customers are routinely given a higher priority than everyone else by using a color-coded system. Each file folder will be noted with a color based on an established hierarchy. The top five major customers will have a unique color. Another color will be reserved for expedited claims, and all remaining customers will share a common color. This system can be implemented immediately and on a running basis. Within 2 weeks, all work in process should have a color associated with it and be prioritized accordingly.

2. **Problem: Claims forwarded to the next operation with incomplete, erroneous, or illegible information.**

   Solution: Starting immediately, we will begin to chart the number of send-backs with each associate's name, then establish a policy that prevents a claim folder from advancing to the next department unless all the information is completed correctly and legibly. We will need to do extensive training to make sure all personnel, in all departments, can accomplish this and catch mistakes and omissions. The time frame for this is about 6 weeks.

3. **Problem: Too much information, which requires additional levels of filtering to get to the information that's needed.**

   Solution: With today's technology, we believe we can scan every document into an optical character reader, then have the computer look for the information that is needed, rather than have an associate read through the entire document. We will need to review the options for a fast-and-accurate scanner, debug the system, and then make sure it is able to find the specific words we need it to find, so it is a 4-month project.

4. **Problem: Lack of communication with customers due to their lack of understanding of technical terminology and/or suspicions of our motivations because of scams.**

   Solution: We will come up with a scripted introduction that will put the customer at ease and assure them we are not trying to deny any claim. We expect to have a psychologist edit the script to make sure we are instilling confidence. Then, we will use a translator to convert our insurance-speak into requests an average person can understand. To do this, we will need to create the translator vocabulary. It will take about a month to research what is currently understood by the public, what colloquial terms apply, and then build the dictionary. Then, it will take 9 months to get it into our software. In the meantime, with some training, the associates can act as translators.

5. **Problem: Delays in common area equipment servicing.**

   Solution: We will need some training here also. I expect we can get the original equipment manufacturer (OEM) to do some and perhaps even recommend a system to ensure we always have the supplies we need to keep working. We cannot be the only company that has this problem, so we might as well talk to the experts and see if they have dealt with similar situations elsewhere.

Summary

Although some of these measures would require extensive training, monitoring, creating information, and depending on outside help, and many are long term, they should all ultimately simplify things. Until each measure is in place, we will depend on the colored priority system outlined in this list to ensure the satisfaction and retention of our major customers. This measure is the fastest and easiest to implement.

I stood up and stretched, walked to the washroom to freshen up, and then headed to Chris's office, ready for the meeting. I gently tapped on the door and nudged it open.

"Hi, Chris. Are you available to review the corrective action plan?" I asked.

"Sure, Pat," came the reply. "Tell me how we're going to turn things around and support all of our customers. I could sure use some good news after the meeting I was just in."

Chris selected a pen and a pad of paper and prepared to listen.

"Yesterday, I gathered everyone in the conference room and had them tell me the issues that were causing problems," I said. "This morning, I sat down and came up with solutions to them all. Here they are."

With that, I handed my plan to Chris, who took a look at it and dwelled on the first item for a while before speaking.

"**Number 1**, frequent reprioritization, which sounds to me like inconsistent assignment and execution of priorities. So, you're telling me that we're going to continue using the current priority policy, but now with a color-coded scheme that will identify important customers and give them special treatment. And, you can get this implemented within 2 weeks. Right?"

I was about to respond but did not get the chance.

"Pat, there's no way this strategy will support all of our customers. It will obviously ignore some of our smaller customers and in a very nonstrategic way. Some of them are growing, and they have the potential to become our most profitable clients only a year or two down the road. You and your department do not have visibility into that. This policy could potentially make our service to these clients *worse*. This won't do. Let's move on to the next problem."

I stood motionless. Already, this was not going well. My first item got shot down, and that was the key to everything.

"**Number 2**, claims forwarded to the next operation with incomplete, erroneous, or illegible information. This is telling me your people won't advance a claim that has incomplete information, and you're going to track and chart who causes the most send-backs. You'll need to train people so they can recognize when information is missing or incomplete, right?"

"Right," I said.

"I'm sorry, Pat, but this won't work either. If we measure how many claims get sent back by each individual, the associates will start selectively working on the easier ones and avoiding the harder ones. This measure will likely contribute to a *longer* overall processing time, not a shorter one."

This meeting is going faster than expected, I thought, as Chris read the next point.

"**Number 3**, too much information, which requires additional levels of filtering to get to the information that's actually needed. You'll have all the incoming information scanned and let a computer determine what's important for processing a claim. Do you realize what that sounds like?"

Apparently not, I thought.

"If a claim has too much information on it, then I don't see how scanning it into a computer will help. Automated word search tools work for Human Resources to eliminate résumés, but that's not our intention here. I don't think we'll save any time, and I think our service to our customers will actually decline and cause more problems—and we've already got plenty, Pat! Plus, what's the time frame here? Will this really begin to resolve our problems quickly? Let's keep going."

"**Number 4**, lack of communication with customers due to their lack of understanding of technical terminology and/or suspicions of our motivations because of scams. So, a scripted introduction will give us credibility and convince our customers we're on their side. And, we'll be able to get all the answers we need because we won't be using insurance-speak, so they'll have no trouble understanding our questions. That's what I'm getting here, right? And we're going to add this vocabulary to the system software, too?"

The sarcasm was so thick I was nearly suffocating on it.

"I do like the idea of translating technical terms into street language, but I don't believe adding them to our software will solve our problems in a timely way. Besides, a 9-month time frame is way too long. We need this done yesterday, so let's see what else there is.

"**Number 5**, delays in common area equipment servicing. The plan here is to have the local distributor manage the supplies and teach us the simple stuff we need to know to keep our equipment functioning."

Chris put down the plan and looked up at me.

"I like the idea of having our local distributor and the OEM do some training and advise us on what other companies are doing to resolve the problems we're having. I believe that's called benchmarking. Maybe we could benchmark the equipment."

Without hesitating, Chris read through the summary and said, "Let's talk about extensive training. Who pays for it, and who minds the store while we train? We need to do it, I know, but it has to be done per some intended, controlled, and sequential impact plan. But, more important, this plan doesn't address how we're going to take care of *all* of our customers, Pat."

I might as well not have even attended this meeting. There was no opportunity to reply to any of Chris's statements. It would have been nice to be heard.

"I think you lost sight of things when you decided to come up with solutions to the issues you and your team found. You came up with good answers to these isolated situations, but they make little impact on the overall problem. To me, the ideas in this plan read like random acts of goodness. Individually, each one has merit, but together, they don't make for an overall solution."

I nodded in agreement, and Chris acknowledged the gesture before continuing. "I can't accept this plan of action because it won't accomplish what we need. You're going to have to make some adjustments to address the needs of all of our customers. Remember to look at the big picture. I think you've got a good grasp of the problem, so what should you do to get back on track? That's rhetorical right now. I suggest you spend the rest of the day and this evening thinking about it, and then we'll talk again tomorrow. Try to look at things from a higher level the next time around and see if that helps."

"Thanks, Chris," I said. "And, uh, thanks for the second chance. During your review of the plan, I wanted to disappear into thin air. But I was able to concentrate enough to recognize that what you were saying was, in fact, a fair assessment—back to square one."

We acknowledged our mutual respect for each other, then I turned and left for my office. For the first time ever, I was glad it was not the one in the corner. I am not sure I could have performed an autopsy on someone's plan as precisely as Chris and still been responsible enough to administer fair criticism while not holding back on any of the deficient proposals.

I spent the rest of the day going over my plan again and attacking some of the backlog that had accumulated on my desk. After a few hours, I decided to leave. My mind seemed to be in a million different places.

As I packed my bag, I was not sure what I was feeling. Certainly, there was the disappointment of a rejected plan, but I was also confused: How had I missed the target so badly? Chris had found little value in my plan and helped me understand it would not fix anything. I was thankful to have been given a second chance to look at the big picture.

I headed out to my car, oblivious to the walk as I went over the past 2 days in my head, the information I had gathered, and how I might regroup. I could not tell you if I passed anyone in the lot or give you a single detail about the weather. I found my car, got behind the wheel, and buckled up. As I drove home, my mind was squarely focused on my own world of problems and what I might do to solve them.

FROM THE AUTHOR

Often, when we map how information flows, we look for areas of opportunity at each process in order to improve. After we note these opportunities, we try to "fix" each process. In other words, we are addressing "point solutions" only. When addressing point solutions, there is no guarantee that the resulting improvements will make a positive impact on the customer. This is because the identified solutions are usually intended to solve bottlenecks or issues that are only symptomatic of underlying causes or that do not relate in any clearly defined way to a system-level design.

It can become a bit like the Whac-A-Mole® carnival game, where we use the Lean and continuous improvement tools available to solve individual problems as they arise. Most point-level fixes are great for solving point-level problems but rarely are they capable of addressing more comprehensive issues like inadequate turnaround times, missed customer promise dates, or excessive turn-backs.

In addition, presenting point-level solutions can often deteriorate into a discussion or debate regarding whether each solution is truly effective. Convincing others of the "correctness" of each idea can be a lengthy process and extremely challenging, as often the ideas cannot be *taught* to other people, only told to them. Solutions also last only as long as the manager or team who thought of them; when these personnel move, the solutions they created tend to dissolve in favor of something else.

5

The Old Friend

It was still early Tuesday evening by the time I got home, but the week already felt like it had lasted an eternity. I seldom had such stressful days—I was not accustomed to tackling a task for which failure might be a realistic outcome—and I was drained of energy. I needed to clear my head so I could think outside the box tomorrow.

I was about to check the refrigerator for some leftovers when my cell phone rang. I did not recognize the number displayed on the screen, which meant I probably did not know the person on the other end. Should I answer it, or just let it go to voice mail? Ignore the phone and maybe the person will go away, I thought.

I looked over the contents of the fridge, but there was nothing too appealing, so I opted to go for takeout. My phone stopped ringing, so at least something was working out as planned. But then, it rang again, and displayed the same number. Maybe it is important, I thought.

"Hello, this is Pat," I said.

"Hi Pat, this is Peyton," came the voice from the other end. "I wasn't sure I had the right number. Are you in the middle of something, or do you have a minute to talk?"

"Oh, hi, Peyton. I didn't recognize the number. What's up?"

"Well, I hate to interrupt your evening, but I have a career decision to make, and I'd appreciate your advice. I was wondering if we could meet for coffee tomorrow morning before work. I remember you told me about your favorite spot on your way to your office, and it isn't far from my commute. Can we meet at 7 a.m.? My treat."

That was all I needed with everything that was going on—something else to drain my brainpower. But, I did wonder what it was all about.

"If you're buying, I'll be there," I replied, attempting to sound cheerful. "I'm actually just figuring out dinner for tonight so I can't chat now, but I'll see you tomorrow."

"Thanks, Pat. See you soon."

"Bye," I said, shutting off the phone. I wondered what Peyton meant by a career decision. Maybe my recruiter had been active again.

I ran out and grabbed a pizza—veggie, for health's sake—and could not shake the feeling from the day as I crawled into bed, exhausted. As I drifted to sleep, my mind kept jumping to different events from the start of the week, and I wondered what Peyton would add to the mix tomorrow.

As Wednesday morning arrived and the sun peeked through a thick layer of clouds, I walked toward the coffeeshop door, entered, and looked around for a remote place where Peyton and I could sit. I always liked to arrive first in any networking meeting so I could pick a seat with a good vantage point. As I checked for open tables, I noticed Peyton was already there.

"Hey, you're early," I said. "And I see you already have your coffee. I'll get mine and be right back."

"Hey, glad you could work this in. By the way, your coffee is already paid for, including Hazel's tip," replied Peyton.

I approached the counter, unsure of what to expect. The line was short, and when it was my turn, Hazel smiled and said, "The usual? Grande latte, two shots of espresso?"

She continued doing the things baristas do to make the morning beverage. "Here you go," she said. "Compliments of your friend. Enjoy."

"OK, I'm impressed," I said, walking back to the table. "What did you have to do to arrange that?"

"Well, it wasn't too hard to imagine you might be recognized here, so when I bought my coffee, I asked if they knew you and what you usually ordered. They did, so I paid them handsomely to take care of you when you arrived."

"Clever," I said, as I sat and scanned the room for anyone I might know who could be a possible interruption. "So, what's the news? I've been wondering ever since you called."

"Well, I shared my career goals with you last week at the conference," said Peyton. "Yesterday, my boss called me in and offered me a supervisory position in the Medicare/Medicaid group, which was my targeted objective. So, now I have a shot at supervising the group that I think I want.

"I also recalled that you had the advantage of observing several management styles before you became a supervisor, and I haven't had that opportunity. I just want to know what you would recommend to help me succeed in this new position. I need to climb a steep learning curve to be able to supervise people the way I want. Are there any good seminars or books you can recommend? I've heard that peer groups can help, too. Are you familiar with any? What do you think about a career coach?"

I felt honored that Peyton was asking me for advice, but after yesterday, I was far less confident that I had anything worth sharing. "Well, first off, congratulations on being offered the supervisor's role," I said. "Are you going to accept it? I think you should go for it, but is there any downside?"

"Yes, I'm going to take it. There's not really any downside, but I *am* a bit concerned, because the performance bar has been set pretty high due to one of our company's other departments. They've been making improvements there over the past few months. I don't know much, but the bulletin board updates in the break room say they've really cut their lead time and improved their ability to meet their promise dates. You know, all that good stuff.

"I don't know if I'll be ready to do that in my group right off the bat, but I know my boss is watching those changes very closely and with a great deal of interest. Our marketing group indicates there's going to be a big increase in our Medicare/Medicaid market segment, which is why management agreed to add a supervisor. So, I'll be accepting a double challenge: learning to be a supervisor while trying to make a breakthrough in the way we perform. My boss has promised to support me, so I'm encouraged about that, at least."

I sat silently and pondered what Peyton said. A department cutting the time it takes to process claims *and* improving its ability to hit promise dates? I wondered how they were doing this.

When I realized Peyton was waiting for a response, I said, "I recommend you take the position with enthusiasm and mention to your boss you'd like to get some mentoring and training in management skills. Your company should offer that support for any internal change in position where different skills are expected. But, most of all, keep your head up and your eyes open to see the big picture at all times."

Do as I say, not as I do, I thought. After another pause and some more contemplation, I decided to confess.

"I have to be honest, though. I don't really feel too qualified to give advice this week. I'm in the middle of a department trend that's not headed in the right direction. I can tell you all about assuming a different position, adapting to a new role with associates that used to be peers, and administering management policy. Been there, done that. But, when performance trends need fixing, apparently, I'm still a novice.

"Things aren't going well at my office. We had a big problem last week while you and I were at that conference. My boss had to get involved and expedite a claim, and it was *still* late. The incident triggered a request for a report from the information technology department, which revealed that our trend in timeliness was bad and getting worse. I got called on the carpet to provide a corrective action plan, which got shot down yesterday. So, I'm back to square one. Like you, I'm determined to find a way forward, but I don't have a clue where to start—at least not yet. That's my challenge for today."

"Wow, now I *am* concerned about taking this position," replied Peyton. "What if I find myself in your shoes? Then what? You'd better figure it out quickly so I can just copy you."

"Well, it sounds like your boss has been watching the improvements in that other department, probably knows the details of their progress, and will provide you some assistance in your own efforts," I said. "I'm sure you'll be fine. Maybe I'll get *my* answer from what *you* implement, so *you'd* better learn fast!"

"I wish I could help."

"Hey, this is your treat and your meeting. We should spend the limited time we have discussing your opportunities. Then, I have to get back to reality."

Peyton sat quietly for a few moments, then said, "I have an idea. Let me ask my boss about the things they did in that other department, and I can let you know how they changed their trend. It's the least I can do."

"I appreciate the help. Thanks, Peyton. And thanks for the coffee. If others are making improvements, then it's possible at my company, too. Speaking of changes, congratulations again on your new position. It seems like it's what you want to do, so it sounds like the right move. It's going to take a lot of effort, but you appear willing to make it work and learn as you go. And, you have a savvy boss who'll support you with what you need."

We simultaneously stood, moved toward the exit, and separated, each to our own vehicle. While still within hearing range, Peyton reiterated, "I'll talk to my boss and call you later today."

"Thanks," I said. "That'd be great. Whatever you can share is appreciated."

Peyton disappeared from sight as I carefully placed the remaining coffee in my cup holder as I got into my car, then headed to work. Soon enough, I found myself in the parking lot, sandwiched between the usual meld of clustered cars, gathering my things, and making my way into my building.

I was excited about what Peyton had told me and was looking forward to what I might find out later in the day. However, I did not know how much I could count on that for today's meeting with Chris. What if Peyton could not convey the plan that department used? What if it was not transferable? It could not be simple, and perhaps it was even proprietary. It would be really frustrating to know a solution existed but not have access to it.

I rode the elevator to my floor, stepped off, and decided to check in with Chris before beginning the day.

"Morning," I said as I got to the door. "I'll check back with you in a few hours, if that's OK. I have some reviewing to do before we meet again to discuss how to improve the timeliness for all of our customers. Does that work for you?"

"Can we make it later, maybe even after lunch? My boss has asked me for a quarterly report this morning, and I'm not sure how long it's going to take to put together, especially since it's not the end of the quarter. I need to project the last month, which sounds a lot like guessing to me."

"No problem, I'll be plenty busy on this project. Let me know when you're ready."

I left and went to my office, then unpacked my bag, sat at my desk, took a deep breath, and decided to look at the big picture.

Where did I go wrong? Most important, I did not have confidence that we could improve the entire customer base, so I narrowed the scope to our major customers. With all of our customers now in mind, maybe I should look at my list of reasons again and reevaluate them. I was not sure this would be any more strategic than what I did the day before, but it was a starting place at least, and I was not really sure what else to do at this point.

I spent some time poring over the list of reasons I had generated, but after an hour or so of thinking about it, I did not feel like I was getting anywhere. I went down to the cafeteria to grab a snack, and when I got back to my office, the phone was ringing. The number on the screen was not familiar to me, and I debated whether I should answer. Curiosity prevailed, however, so I accepted the call.

"Hello, this is Pat."

"Hey, this is Peyton. Do you have a few minutes to talk? I have something I think you'd like to hear."

I was glad I answered my phone.

"Sure. But first, did you accept the offer?"

"Yes, I did, but that's not why I'm calling. I spoke to my boss about the department that's making all the improvements. It's claims processing for our industrial market. Different than what you do, but similar enough, I suspect. They handle policies that include buildings, liability, fleet insurance—stuff like that. I asked if I could get some understanding of what they did to improve their performance so I could share it with you and, get this: I was told that I had been invited—actually, *expected*—to become familiar with their efforts because they want me to replicate the results in the Medicare/Medicaid group. How about that!"

"That's great," I replied, although I actually felt a bit deflated—waiting for Peyton's report was not going to help me in a timely fashion. "Did you find out what they do differently?"

"No, not yet. There's a good news, bad news element to this call. First, the bad news. I tried to find out what changes they made so I could relay the information to you. My boss told me they were all commonsense changes but would take too long to explain. Instead, he arranged for me to spend some time in that department to see for myself what they do differently, which will then be followed by training and some mentoring."

"Good for you," I said. "I guess I *will* have to learn everything from you but, unfortunately, not soon enough. I still don't have any insight on what to do here."

I was really disappointed. If a department could accomplish such a turn-around, then there had to be a strategy that worked, and it might be applicable to my situation. I desperately wanted to know what they did, and I thought Peyton would be able to tell me.

"You mentioned a good news element, too. Care to elaborate on that?"

"Oh, that's right. I did, didn't I? What do you have planned for tomorrow? Can you break away from your work to accompany me on the orientation? The group feels very confident about their progress and is willing to act as a benchmark for other companies. I asked if you could join me and, since our companies don't compete in the same market, both my boss and the industrial market department manager agreed to have you come. They think it'll be good for the associates in the department to talk about the differences between how they do things now and how they used to do them. They feel they'll gain confidence in their progress and actually recognize how far they've come. Can you make it?"

"Wow, give me a minute to understand this offer. You're telling me that tomorrow, I'm going to be allowed to enter your company and participate in a benchmarking tour, where I'll learn about the changes your industrial market department has made, bring that knowledge and information back with me, and then apply it? Is that what you're asking? Yes, of course I want to go, but I'll have to clear it with my boss. When do you need to know?"

"Actually, I anticipated that you would be coming, so I tentatively committed for you. You should come by at 8 a.m. tomorrow. I'll give you directions later. When you get here, go to the front lobby, sign in, and someone will come out to meet you. The tour could take the whole day, and we're counting on you asking a lot of questions. With you probing to understand how and why things have changed, the associates will have to explain it to you, and they'll better realize their own understanding. So, we gain from this as well."

"Thanks," I said. "I'll let you know if there's some reason I won't be able to make it, but I can't imagine what could keep me away. If needed, should I call you at this number or your cell?"

"Call my cell," replied Peyton. "I don't expect to be spending much time at my desk in the next 2 weeks."

"Thanks, Peyton," I said. "I owe you one. I sure am glad we met up at that conference last week."

This could be the breakthrough I needed to get things moving. I *had* to do this the next day, no question.

As I was musing over my newfound fortune, I suddenly realized that Chris needed to know about the plan and agree to it. I began to generate a document that would illustrate the importance of this opportunity. It took some time, but when I was done, I had something I was confident would do the trick.

It was near enough to when we were supposed to meet, so I printed my document and headed to Chris's office, stopping in the doorway and waiting to be noticed. After a moment, Chris looked up and said, "Hi, Pat. I was just thinking about you. How's it going? Have you made any breakthroughs?"

"My new plan is to copy another company's success," I blurted out. Well, nothing like cutting to the chase.

"Let me try that again."

I handed Chris the document, then realized I did the same thing yesterday before promptly losing control of the meeting. Determined to be a participant in this one, I said, "Let me take you through the list and offer my thoughts as we go."

Not waiting for approval, I began to read: "The original plan didn't work because, one, we lost sight of the big picture, and two, we had the wrong scope and focused only on our major customers."

I stopped reading from the list and added, "So, the scope was inappropriately limited because I wasn't confident we could accomplish what we need to. I've changed my thinking about that and realize now that we're going to have to figure out how to handle all of our customers."

Chris nodded, and I continued.

"I reviewed my list of reasons, but I was unable to come up with any additional insights. Last week, I attended a conference and reconnected with an old college acquaintance, who works at another company with similar processes to ours where they've made great progress in both the time it takes to process claims and their ability to hit their promise dates."

"OK, I'm listening," said Chris.

"We can determine how feasible it is for us to implement a similar process," I said. "Can it be done here? I hope so, yes. Tomorrow, I'll be allowed to benchmark that company's processes and gain exposure to what they do."

"That sounds fine," said Chris. "I agree you have a great opportunity to benchmark another company, and there's no crime in copying what works."

"So, I have your approval to go tomorrow?" I asked, a little surprised.

"Yes, most certainly. I hope you find something there you can bring back and apply. But, if you don't, we can discuss other options. I have confidence in you, Pat. That's why I hired you 8 months ago, and that's why I'm keeping you on this project."

"Thanks, Chris," I said. "Anything else?"

"Nope, that'll do it. Let's meet on Friday to review what you find tomorrow."

"Sounds good," I said. "See you then."

Now *that* was a good meeting, I thought as I left the room. I was able to participate, and Chris was supportive. I guess I tend to be more convincing when my arguments have some substance to them. I had to let Peyton know I was confirmed for the next day.

I called Peyton's cell phone and got no answer, so I left a voice mail stating I would be in the lobby by 8 o'clock on Thursday morning. Later that afternoon, Peyton called back to let me know the best route to the company considering the construction, traffic patterns, and road conditions. It was a nice touch, and it left me feeling upbeat at the end of the day. I packed up, grabbed my driving directions, and left the office, excited for the next day.

FROM THE AUTHOR

A common approach utilized by companies to solve their problems is to benchmark what others have done. It seems like a logical strategy: If other organizations have faced similar problems, it makes sense to visit them and see what they did to solve them. Once the visit is complete, the attendees then take what worked at the host organization and apply it at their own business.

While benchmarking tours can be useful in helping companies gain insight on how other companies addressed issues and solved specific problems, they can also drive a "cut-and-paste" mentality that can have limited value when attempting to design a complete system of information flow. In this mentality, the thinking would be, "We need a visual board just like that." Rather than look for solutions, a good benchmarking visit asks *why* a company did what it did, takes a deep dive into the process used, and examines how the company approached improvement.

Complicating matters further is that on a typical benchmarking tour, the participants are only able to observe the *results* of what was done. It is often challenging to see (as in physically see with your eyes) the process that was applied to achieve those results. It is also usually difficult to observe or understand any iteration that had to transpire to achieve the finalized state that is being showcased on the benchmarking tour. Normally, the only iteration available to the benchmarking participants is the one currently in use during the normal day-to-day running of the business; the other iterations that came before it have been either refined or eliminated.

A good benchmarking tour would include an educational component with the tour, preferably before the tour. The more information flow-level education that can be taught, the better, as this enables the attendees to understand the rationale behind *why* the process was applied in certain ways, not just how it was applied.

With this understanding, participants can then also identify key differences between their businesses and work out how to adapt the process when they go to implement it at their own business. This makes it less likely that attendees will attempt to "fit a square peg into a round hole" by trying to apply solutions that simply will not work at their organizations. Instead, providing information flow-level education and understanding the principles and guidelines used increases the likelihood that there will be tangible takeaways from the benchmarking tour, ones that can then be applied by the participants at their own organizations for positive results.

6

The Fateful Day

The alarm clock rang with its usual annoying sound, but I was in a light slumber and welcomed the command to get out of bed. I had slept well, but in heavy anticipation of what was to come today. I had to admit: I was excited about what I might discover.

Methodically, I executed my morning routine and headed out the door. I really did not know what to expect that day, but if the department Peyton talked about truly improved its performance, then I should be able to learn some of what they did and implement it at my office.

These people process industrial claims, I thought. That could not be as difficult as medical claims. I was sure we had more clients, more procedures, and—because we dealt with individuals rather than businesses—more incorrect or missing information. But, I hoped there would be enough similarities that I would learn something of value.

I arrived at Peyton's company shortly before 8 a.m., parked in a visitor's space, locked my car, and then found my way into the lobby. I noticed the LED monitor on the wall scrolling information about the company, the weather, associate announcements, and then my name on the welcome screen. This was impressive, especially because I was not even a paying customer.

I approached the sign-in desk, where I was greeted in a friendly tone and asked if I was Pat O'Malley. After confirming, I signed in and received a visitor's badge. The receptionist then placed a call and informed the person on the other end that their visitor had arrived.

Shortly after, a woman approached me with an extended hand. We shook, and she introduced herself as Jennifer Carrson, informing me she was the continuous improvement manager and would be escorting me to the conference room to meet with Peyton, after which the three of us would spend the day learning about the system they had implemented.

As we made our way down the hallway, Jennifer said they had chosen the industrial claims processing team to pilot their improvements. When I asked her why, she said, "Why don't we talk about that when we meet with Peyton?"

I nodded as she continued. "Peyton told me you two reconnected at a conference last week, and that you're experiencing some of the same problems we faced before we began to think differently about how we do things. Perhaps we can help."

I smiled for a second, then reality kicked in, and my expression changed. "Well, I hope so," I said. "But I came back to a bit of a mess after the conference."

Jennifer half smiled and said, "It always seems to happen that way, doesn't it? I used to never take more than a long weekend off for fear of what I would come back to. But things are a little smoother here now, so I was able to work in a trip to Florida for spring break with my family this year."

"So, why are things running smoother now?" I asked, waiting to hear the secret to their success.

"It's simple," she said. "We learned about true flow and figured out how to apply it to our business to create Operational Excellence. It requires a little different perspective on things. You'll find out about that along with Peyton this morning, then I have some people I want you to meet this afternoon—the ones who are actually doing the work. We'll discuss everything beforehand, but I think it's better if you also see the system for yourself and hear how it works from the people who operate it."

As we left the lobby and walked through the office, Jennifer pointed out directions to the conference area, as well as the locations of nearby break rooms, restrooms, and water fountains. Each of these areas was clearly marked with international symbols. As we neared the conference room, I noticed the hallways were identified with team names, and there were color-themed variations in certain clusters of cubicles. I did not see any of the typical departmental names posted, however.

"Here we are," said Jennifer. "Good morning, Peyton. How are you today?"

"Morning, Jennifer. And to you, Pat. Glad you could rearrange your schedule so quickly to be here. I know you'll have some good questions that I wouldn't even think of asking."

"I have those questions right here, ready to start," I said, lifting my bag.

"We'll be starting in about 5 minutes. I have to retrieve some materials from the copy center," said Jennifer. "Make yourselves comfortable and feel free to review the agenda in front of you. There's some coffee, tea, and chilled water in the nearby break area, so help yourselves. And, get ready to learn a new language."

"A new language?" I said to Peyton after she had left the room. "I was never good at foreign languages. I'm not even that good with English! I just need to know how to solve my problems. Am I on the wrong bus here?"

"Relax," said Peyton. "Last night, I was reading some material Jennifer gave me, and it implied that we're going to have to get familiar with a new way of thinking. I'm sure that's all she means."

As we were reviewing the agenda, Jennifer returned.

"Great, I see you're already showing interest in what we'll be doing today!" she said. "So let's get started. The day's format will be structured but informal, so ask questions whenever you find something confusing. We're going to build on each element we discuss, so it's important to grasp each step as we go through it. Pat, I understand you have department management experience and are currently trying to solve some problems, but with a different approach. I'm going to depend on you to point out the differences in our system, for the benefit of both you and Peyton. It's hard to appreciate some of the subtle contrasts without a reference point, so I'm hoping you can provide that baseline. OK?"

"Sounds good," I said.

"All right, let me give you some background on industrial claims processing," said Jennifer, and with that, she quickly summarized the background, problem, scope, and schedule of their project. It seemed their previous decline in performance was similar to what my department was currently experiencing. The management team had heard about Operational Excellence and decided to apply the principles in their worst performing area so their efforts would produce the greatest results for the overall business. The logic was that if they could achieve Operational Excellence there, it would be a model that could be used to teach the rest of the company.

"Peyton, you and Pat are probably going to hear some unfamiliar terms over the course of the day, but bear with me," said Jennifer. "When this whole process started about 4 months ago, I didn't know much about continuous improvement or which companies were famous for being really good at it. I was something of a newbie. But, I quickly got a solid education in the principles of Operational Excellence, then it fell on me to educate the team that actually applied the methodology. After all was said and done, life got simpler and better for everyone, including the boss.

"And, speaking of the boss, one of the first things we had to do was get our management group aligned, and that was no easy task. I found a great speaker on Operational Excellence who was appearing at a conference, so I convinced our chief executive officer and other executives to attend the session. When they returned, they were so excited about what they heard they couldn't wait to get started.

"By this point, we all understood the end game of Operational Excellence, but we felt we needed some help getting started with the process. We found someone who was an expert in teaching Operational Excellence in the business process environment, and that office-specific knowledge enabled us to accelerate our success as opposed to performing random acts of goodness. That's where I got my education."

Random acts of goodness—that was not the first time I had heard that phrase.

"We might be on a journey," continued Jennifer, "but that *doesn't* mean we don't have a destination. Ours is Operational Excellence, and knowing where we were going enabled us to get there a lot faster. It was like we had a GPS device to always keep us on course. I believe we've accomplished more and come farther, faster in the past 4 months than many companies have in the past 4 *years*.

"What does that mean? Most companies see continuous improvement as using tools to get better every day, or they try to eliminate waste wherever they can find it."

Jennifer went to the flip chart and drew a graph (Figure 6.1). "Typically, we improve a little bit, then we sustain at that level, and we keep going like this. Don't get me wrong: It's all good; it just takes a long time."

She drew another graph on the flip chart to illustrate her point (Figure 6.2). "But, Operational Excellence raises the bar," said Jennifer, bringing another graph to life (Figure 6.3).

"With Operational Excellence as our destination, we can do more, and do it faster, than even some of the best companies," she said. When she added a little more detail to the graph, it became clear to me that we could go much further, sooner, by striving for Operational Excellence (Figure 6.4).

"OK, hold on a second," said Peyton. "What exactly is Operational Excellence? You've mentioned it a few times now, and even said it's the destination of our journey. But, how is Operational Excellence different from any other corporate catchphrase out there?"

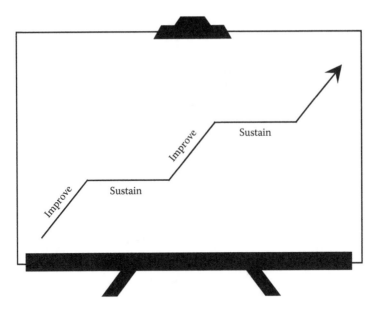

FIGURE 6.1
The staircase of continuous improvement: Tools are used to eliminate waste and get a little better every day.

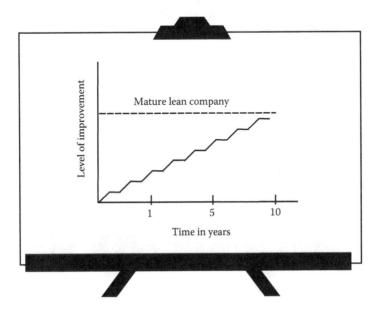

FIGURE 6.2
The improve/sustain method of improvement *does* achieve results, but it usually takes many years.

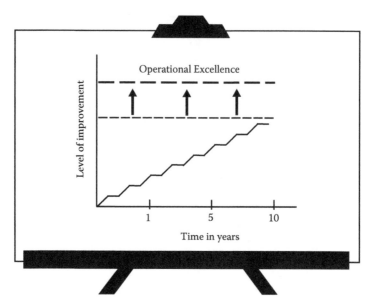

FIGURE 6.3

Operational Excellence raises the ceiling of our continuous improvement efforts.

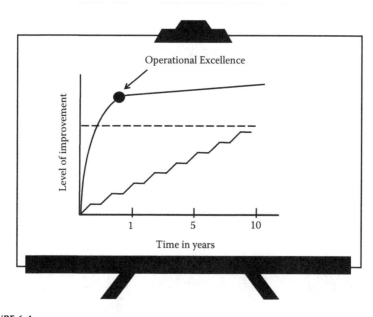

FIGURE 6.4

Operational Excellence takes us much farther, much faster than traditional continuous improvement approaches.

"Yes, how do you define it?" I added. "We talk about Operational Excellence at my company. We even have a metrics board that measures safety, productivity, delivery, and customer satisfaction. It announces updates in our quality improvement programs, suggestions, rewards, recognitions, and numerous employment benefits for self-improvement."

Jennifer nodded and said, "I'll define Operational Excellence now because it's so critical to what we're going to be doing today. But, the definition will probably have deeper meaning for you once you actually see Operational Excellence in action later, so you might want to write it down.

"**Operational Excellence** is when each and every employee can *see the flow of value* to the customer and *fix that flow before* it breaks down."

She then explained that the goal is to have value flow continuously to the customer, uninterrupted, and to have frontline employees be able to identify when the flow of value is starting to break down, step in, correct it, and get it back on track. I was a little confused at first because I did not know *what* we flow in an office, so I asked and Jennifer replied that we typically flow knowledge and information as opposed to something physical or tangible, although this was also possible.

With that question out of the way, I thought about everything for a minute, and then it became clear. I could immediately see the power of Jennifer's definition of Operational Excellence. It was simple, easy to understand, powerful, practical, and applicable at all levels of an organization; these last two details were particularly key. Because the definition was not just some lofty slogan, I could easily picture myself discussing Operational Excellence with frontline employees and upper management alike because it was something to which they could all relate.

"All right," said Jennifer. "Now, I want you both to imagine a world where you never have to worry about whether your jobs are on time, everyone is always working on the right thing, there are never any priority shifts, and your jobs always get out to your customers when they're supposed to. Oh, and by the way, all of your work flows through the office *without any management intervention whatsoever.* What would you say to that?"

Obviously, I was extremely skeptical of such a scenario. It would be amazing if I could do any one of those things in my office, but to think of them all happening without management intervention—no way. I suddenly wondered if I was going to get anything useful out of today's session. Everything Jennifer just said sounded like pie-in-the-sky foolishness that could not be applied to the unique, complex situation I faced at my company.

"Well," I said, "I think I would say two things. One, everything you described sounds amazing. And, two, it sounds like a total fantasy, especially the part about no management intervention."

"That's a natural reaction at this point, Pat, because we haven't covered much about Operational Excellence," replied Jennifer. "But, I think it'll make more sense once I explain why it's possible for anyone to achieve Operational Excellence.

"Striving for and achieving Operational Excellence is not about having the right leader. It's about following the right process and using the right guidelines. We're not going to rely on personal opinions to get us there or the decisions of managers. We're going to use a process, because a process can be taught to everyone, and good opinions cannot. That's why anyone can strive for Operational Excellence, in *any* environment, and make it happen.

"By using a process that we teach to everyone, we won't and don't need managers making decisions all the time. In fact, our managers won't have time, because with Operational Excellence, they'll be busy doing something else entirely. I'll talk more about that later, but for now, know that management has a very specific and important role to play when it comes to Operational Excellence, one that will benefit the entire business and keep management focused on what matters most."

I was now more intrigued. When Jennifer talked about striving for Operational Excellence by following a process and not simply relying on effective or clever leaders, she got my attention. I have known too many people who worked at companies that were successful only because the leader carried a bigger hammer than everyone else. Then, when that person left, everything fell apart. But, if I could transform my office by teaching a process to everyone, I could create change that would last, no matter who left or joined the company.

"OK," said Jennifer. "Today's all about getting an overview of Operational Excellence and what process you need to follow to achieve it in the office. I'm going to be brief, so keep in mind there's more to it than what I'm going to be able to get into today. To keep things relatively simple, we're going to take the definition of Operational Excellence and break it down into two parts. Remember, the full definition is that each and every employee can see the flow of value to the customer and fix that flow before it breaks down. Let's start with the first part of the definition about each and every employee seeing the flow of value to the customer. What do you think we should talk about first?"

"It seems to me the first thing we need to discuss is value," I said. "What it is and how we should define it. If part of Operational Excellence is flowing value to the customer, then we'd better know what we're talking about."

"Very good," said Jennifer, as she moved to the front of the room and stood by the easel. "So, what's value? What do you think?"

"Something worth paying for," answered Peyton. "If I'm a customer, then I'm willing to pay for goods and services that hold value for me."

"That's good, Peyton," responded Jennifer. "Actually, it's really close. But we're after something a little more specific. When we talk about value in an office setting, we're referring to any business process *activity* the customer is willing to pay for (Womack and Jones 1996, p. 311). Value was first coined in this way through its use in Lean."

"How's that any different from what I said?" asked Peyton.

"It all comes down to the word *activity*," said Jennifer. "The customer doesn't necessarily want to pay for anything and everything we do, only for the specific activities that generate a product or service for them. For example, the physical act of printing a check adds value, but meetings to talk about a customer's claims do not. Think of value as the actions, or verbs, in our business processes that the customer is willing to pay for. Anything that does not add value is waste. Bear in mind there are activities that do not add value but that we have to do anyway due to technological limitations or legal mandates. Any questions on value?"

Neither Peyton nor I had any lingering uncertainties, so Jennifer continued.

"Now that we know what we're talking about when we use the word *value*, we're going to go over a quick example that will illustrate the first part of our Operational Excellence definition and demonstrate how we're able to see the *flow* of value. Would you mind rearranging your seats for me?"

Jennifer had us sit side by side and then joined us at the conference table. Peyton was in the middle, I was on the right, and Jennifer was on the left. To Peyton's left and right, she put a large *X* (Figure 6.5).

FIGURE 6.5
Jennifer, Peyton, and Pat seated at a conference table.

"I have a number of documents that require your approval, which are these blank sheets here," said Jennifer, holding up some squares of paper. "Each of us will review a document to ensure the prior approval is legible, approve it by initialing it, and then place it on the X to our right, where it will be picked up and processed by the next person. We can only place a job on the X when the space opens up. So, if another job happens to be on the X when you go to put yours there, you can't do it. It should only take about 2 seconds for each of us to sign our names. And, Pat, when you're done signing yours, just pile up the sheets to your right. Any questions?"

Peyton and I understood what we'd heard, so we started the exercise and worked silently for a short amount of time. By the time we finished, I had accumulated a fair number of papers to my right (Figure 6.6).

"All right, good job everyone," said Jennifer. "What we've just created is something called a continuous flow processing cell, or a one-piece flow cell. In this type of setup, we operate in a process one, move one fashion. So, each person only works on one job at a time, and when done with it, they move it on to the next person. We're going to cover continuous flow in much more detail in just a bit, but for right now, I'm showing it to you for a slightly different purpose. Peyton, I need to ask you some questions about your role in the exercise we just did."

With that, Jennifer got up from her chair and proceeded to write five questions on the flip chart at the front of the room (Figure 6.7).

Pointing to the easel, Jennifer said, "Peyton, can you answer all of these questions?"

After thinking about it for a few moments, Peyton said, "Yes, I think so. Let me take them one at a time just to be sure. The first one's easy. I knew what to work on next based on whatever you handed me. For question 2, I got my work from you. More specifically, I retrieved it from the X on my left. For question 3, you told us before the exercise started that it should only take about 2 seconds to complete a job, so that was clear. For question 4, I sent my work to Pat. Specifically, I sent my work to the X on my

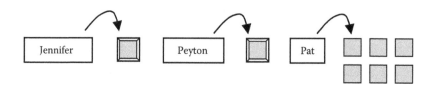

FIGURE 6.6

The arrangement of papers on the conference table at the conclusion of the exercise.

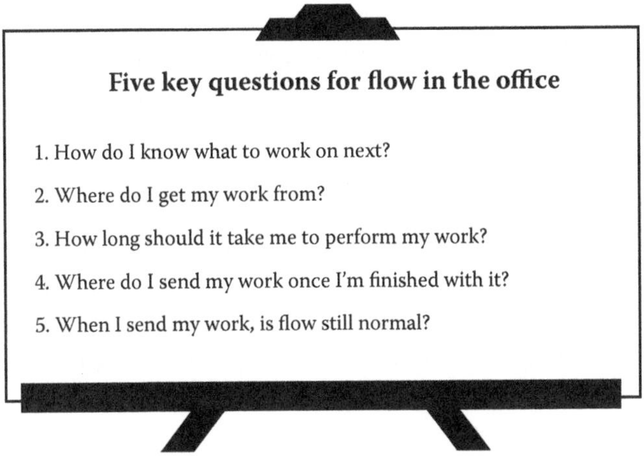

Five key questions for flow in the office

1. How do I know what to work on next?

2. Where do I get my work from?

3. How long should it take me to perform my work?

4. Where do I send my work once I'm finished with it?

5. When I send my work, is flow still normal?

FIGURE 6.7
The five key questions for flow in the office.

right, and Pat took it from there. For the last question, that's a bit trickier, but I think flow was normal every time I sent my work to Pat. The X was always open on the table, so that means flow was always normal. If the X had been occupied, then that would have told me flow was abnormal because Pat wasn't taking and completing work at the appropriate pace to keep up with me and you."

"Very good!" said Jennifer. "See how easy that was? If we can correctly answer these five questions, then we have the basis for good flow. As long as one more condition is met, we're well on our way to achieving Operational Excellence: There can't be any managers, supervisors, schedules, or computer printouts telling each person what to do next."

That last statement caused Peyton and I to take notice because it seemed unfathomable an office could ever work like that, but Jennifer went on. "Before you think I'm completely crazy, let me ask you this. How many managers, supervisors, or computer printouts did we need for our continuous flow cell to work?"

"None!" said Peyton, and the proverbial lightbulb also went on over my head.

"Exactly," said Jennifer. "Everything in the continuous flow processing cell happened without management intervention—none whatsoever. No one hovering over us, no reports telling us what to do next. And since we don't need schedules, we don't have to spend time creating them. Imagine if your company could function as seamlessly as our continuous flow cell did."

She paused to give us time to think about it, and I sat in my seat mulling over everything. With a clear example to reference, I now had a better understanding of what Jennifer meant earlier when she spoke of work flowing through the office without management intervention. But, something else was bothering me, so I spoke up.

"I understand the exercise we just did, but I don't really see the point of it. It's way too simple. Nothing in the office, or at least my office, works like this. How is it supposed to help us?"

"You're absolutely right," said Jennifer, somewhat to my surprise. "The exercise was simple, but it was designed that way to illustrate a very specific point. First, I'm sure you'd agree that Peyton answered all five questions satisfactorily, right?"

"Yes," I said, not really sure where she was going with this.

"And I'm sure you'd also agree that the three of us operated successfully with absolutely no management intervention, right?" she asked.

"Yes," I said. "I'd agree with that, too."

"Good," she said. "Then you're one step closer to understanding what it is we're trying to achieve with Operational Excellence. This continuous flow cell worked because everyone in it was *connected* to one another. You, Peyton, and I were connected in flow, and we knew we had flow because we were able to answer those five questions. In addition, we were able to function without management intervention of any kind. What we're going to do now is take the same concepts that made this whole thing work and expand them throughout the entire office to flow information and capture knowledge, which are the two key functions of an office."

"You mean we're going to seat everybody side by side?" I asked, incredulous.

Jennifer laughed. "No, not quite. The goal will be for every employee in the office to be connected in flow, able to answer all five questions, and function without management intervention. But, because the office is much more complicated than the simple exercise we just did, the process we're going to use will be different and more involved, and that's exactly what we're going to get into next."

FROM THE AUTHOR

Rather than looking at an office and trying to improve it through an endless journey of waste elimination, having a destination of Operational Excellence will enable the company to move its office performance from point A to point B. Setting a destination allows us to build a road map to achieve it as well. Therefore, the journey will not be endless and obscure; it will have focus, a destination, and a step-by-step process to achieve the destination, usually in months rather than years.

While flow is one of the founding concepts to achieve Operational Excellence, flow in the office is a difficult concept. We cannot line up everyone and form an assembly line. Everyone is usually shared among several duties. The five questions for flow help us understand how to establish flow through all the activities that occur in the office.

The exercise demonstrated in this chapter and the accompanying five questions for flow provide the end goal of Operational Excellence in a practical way. Everyone in the example always knew what to work on next without having to ask any questions or seek any supervisors, and everyone could easily see if the flow was normal or abnormal just by looking.

Although real-life offices are much more complex than this exercise, the basic tenets of what we are trying to achieve are the same: Create a system that flows information and captures knowledge where each employee always knows what to work on next *from the flow*. At its most fundamental level, this is what enables us to achieve Operational Excellence.

It might sound difficult to do this given how many responsibilities employees typically have, but designing up front how the end-to-end flow will operate ensures that these multiple responsibilities are accounted for in the design. When beginning to implement Operational Excellence in your office, the end goal is to design a flow of information that answers the five questions for flow at every activity by establishing connections between them. To do this, however, we will need to use some techniques and guidelines that are more innovative, which are covered in the next two chapters.

7

The Education, Part I

Jennifer stood by the easel and said, "Like we talked about before, we're breaking down the definition of Operational Excellence into two parts. We've already talked a little bit about how to see the flow of value. But, to do that, we need to have flow first, don't we?"

Peyton and I both nodded.

"Glad you agree," said Jennifer. "So, if you two were going to try to create flow in your offices, what would you do?"

I thought about it for a few moments before saying, "I'm not sure what you mean. It sounds like creating flow will make things better, so I think I'd just go about it in my normal way."

"What way is that?" asked Jennifer.

"Well, I'd pull my team together in a room, set some goals and objectives, and do some brainstorming," I began. "After enough time and good ideas, we'd decide on the best ones."

"I thought you might respond with something like that," said Jennifer. "Most companies do just what you described, but that's *exactly* what we're *not* going to do. Setting goals and objectives and brainstorming work great for some things, but not for creating flow in the office and achieving Operational Excellence."

"Wait a minute," I replied. "We do a lot of brainstorming at my company. We always want everyone's input and knowledge. It's part of our culture to solicit everyone's ideas."

Jennifer didn't budge. "Yes," she said. "That's the common approach, and it's one of the major game changers in Operational Excellence."

"All right," I conceded. "If brainstorming is out, then what do we do?"

"I'm glad you asked," said Jennifer. "For the rest of the morning, I'm going to briefly describe the sequence of steps we applied to create flow in our office. Peyton, you'll get more in-depth training on this in the days to come, but for now, I just want both of you to be aware of the process we used. After we understand these steps, we'll go out into the office and observe them in action. I'll point out the areas that were transformed and give the associates a chance to explain how everything works and to answer any questions you may have. The exercise will benefit everyone because when the associates explain what they do, they'll be reinforcing their understanding of Operational Excellence and building confidence in the new system. Let's get started."

With that, Jennifer went to the front of the room and stood by the easel. She picked up a marker and flipped to a new page.

"We use nine guidelines to create flow in our business processes," said Jennifer. "I'll list them all, and so should you. I've found that writing things down helps people retain what they're learning."

She listed the nine guidelines on the page (Figure 7.1). "Like I said before, we're leaving out some steps that you must—I repeat—*must* go through if you're going to strive for Operational Excellence," said Jennifer. "But I won't go into them now because we don't have enough time. Plus, today we're just trying to get an understanding of the process and methodology involved.

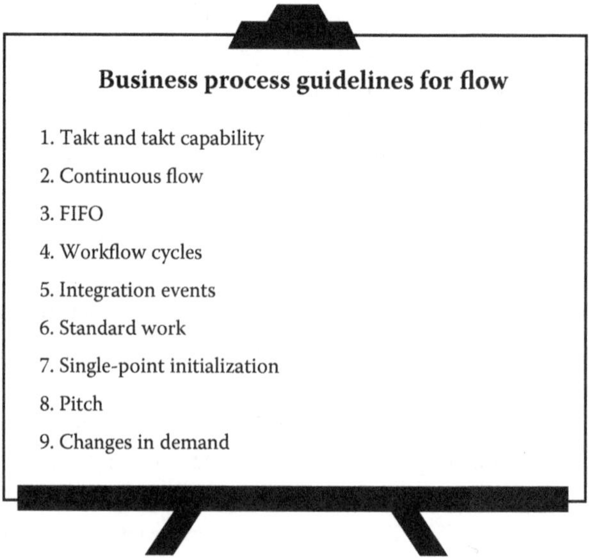

Business process guidelines for flow

1. Takt and takt capability
2. Continuous flow
3. FIFO
4. Workflow cycles
5. Integration events
6. Standard work
7. Single-point initialization
8. Pitch
9. Changes in demand

FIGURE 7.1
The nine business process guidelines for flow.

"Have you written down the guidelines? These represent a disciplined, scientific, sequential approach to creating flow. We use the first six to design our flow, and we use the last three guidelines to determine how we're going to operate it. These guidelines are to be used in sequence, not as a menu. We can't just pick and choose which ones to use, and we don't brainstorm. This will make more sense as I explain each guideline and show how they build on one another to create flow."

TAKT AND TAKT CAPABILITY

"Takt and takt capability are going to tell us how often we need to process and complete work in the office. First, though, we need to figure out what the demand profile looks like for a particular product or service delivered by the office."

Jennifer drew some quick sketches on the flip chart (Figure 7.2). "The demand profile could look like one of these sketches, it could look fairly steady state, or it could look nothing like these. Either way, we need to determine what the demand profile looks like and identify if there is any variation. If there is, we need to look at what's causing it.

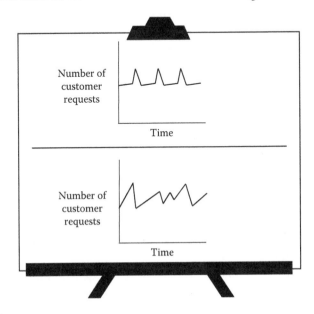

FIGURE 7.2
Two examples of demand profiles.

"For example, with industrial claims processing, we did some analysis and found that the greatest demand was always on Friday. Essentially, our demand profile looked like the one I drew in the upper portion of the flip chart. After some digging, we determined that this variation was self-induced. Some people were just waiting until the end of the week to flush their work to us. So, with a little education and communication, we were able to eliminate some of that variation. Now, we didn't remove *all* of it because some was truly out of our control, but this went a long way toward smoothing out the peaks and valleys.

"Once we have a demand profile for the service, the next step is to create a *takt capability* for it. This is a measurement of how much volume *and mix* we can produce over a given time period, not just volume like we might see with traditional capacity models. The mix is the critical addition here, and it refers to the different types of jobs we might receive from the customer. In our case, it's different types of claims. We know that certain claims take longer than others, so if the mix of claims changes, then it's going to affect how much work we can do within a given time period."

"But I don't see how this really helps us," I said. "Even if we're able to determine a takt capability, we won't know exactly what our customers are going to request from us on any given day."

"That's an important point, Pat," said Jennifer. "Because we won't know exactly how many requests we're going to receive from our customers on any given day, we want to establish not just one takt capability, but *multiple* takt capabilities. Each takt capability accommodates a specific range of volume and mix we might receive. We might not know what the customer is going to send to us each day, but we should be able to determine the volume and mix we're capable of completing each day. It would look something like this." Jennifer flipped to a new page and sketched a new drawing (Figure 7.3).

"The first takt capability needs to be able to satisfy 80% of normal conditions, but we'll probably need one for peak demand times and maybe even another one for times when demand is way down to make sure we don't have too many people working on things that aren't very urgent."

"OK, that makes sense," said Peyton. "I wouldn't think we could have a one-size-fits-all approach."

"No, probably not," said Jennifer. "Once we determine the takt capabilities we're going to use, we then need to determine a takt time for each capability. This will tell us how fast work needs to be completed to ensure we meet the established takt capability."

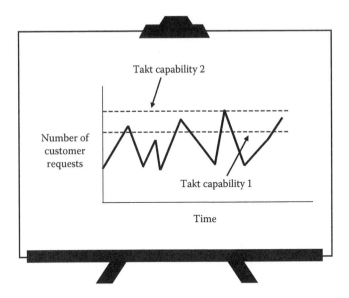

FIGURE 7.3
Two takt capabilities created for a demand profile.

"Do we calculate takt in this case like we would in every other?" I asked.

"Yes," said Jennifer. "I think you're referring to what I'm thinking of, but it can get a little tricky in the office, so let me sketch it on the flip chart just to make sure" (Figure 7.4). "Here's how we compute our takt time," said Jennifer, pointing to the flip chart. "Peyton, how many effective working hours do we have in a day?"

"Theoretically, we're in the building 9 hours per day, but many people are here for much longer," replied Peyton.

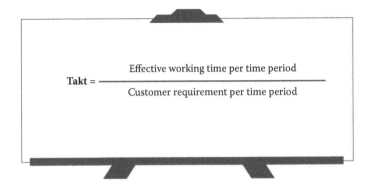

FIGURE 7.4
The equation used for determining takt time.

"Right, but how many of those scheduled hours do you actually spend working on specific jobs like claims?"

"Well, based on what we just covered, it would depend on the takt capability we set, wouldn't it?" asked Peyton.

"That's right," said Jennifer. "Pat, this is what I meant earlier when I said this could get a bit tricky in the office. The equation for determining takt time still works, but the available time is going to be dictated by the takt capability we're using. So, we might not have a full day to work on claims. Maybe it's only 2 hours a day or 4 hours a day, and this will affect how we create a takt time for each takt capability because the available time isn't quite so set in stone. Does this make sense?"

"I think so," I said. "As long as we're following the right process for setting up takt capabilities, I think we'll stay out of trouble."

"Yes," said Jennifer. "And be sure to review the takt capabilities periodically to determine if they need to be recalculated so you're not caught flat-footed if the demand profile starts looking different.

"This afternoon, on the tour, you'll see a system that shows our associates when their volume and mix of work has exceeded their takt capability, and you'll also see how they react and fix the flow before it breaks down—all *without* management intervention. That brings us back to Operational Excellence, but we'll save that for when we get to the second part of the definition.

"If there aren't any other questions, then let's move on to the next guideline."

CONTINUOUS FLOW

"The next guideline is continuous flow," said Jennifer. "We won't be able to cover all the details of this one today, but there are plenty of books out there that can help fill in the gaps for you. We saw continuous flow once before during our signature exercise when we demonstrated how to see the flow of value. Because most people in the office are shared resources and divide their time among many different duties and responsibilities, full-time continuous flow isn't really a viable option. But, we can have *part-time* continuous flow, where the associates involved all have the same amount of work to do, perform to a takt time, and operate in process one, move one fashion.

"Let's think back to the exercise we did. What's it like in our offices now, when we don't have continuous flow?"

"Work piles up everywhere," I said. "And not just at the end of the line like it did in the signature exercise. All those in-baskets on everyone's desks or e-mail inboxes are filled to the brim with work that needs to get done."

"Good," replied Jennifer. "What happens to the work while it sits in between everyone? Just to be clear, even though the in-baskets sit on people's desks, no single associate has ownership of the work in them. The work is in limbo. At that point, it doesn't belong to the person who put it there any more or less than it does to the person who will eventually take it. So, let me ask you this: What happens or can happen to work while it's waiting to be processed?"

"Well, it can be sorted and shuffled," I offered. "Priorities might change. Sometimes, the work requires a more in-depth review because it's gone cold sitting for so long. Or, a customer's needs have changed, and we don't know it."

"All good responses, Pat, but I'll answer my own question to drive home the point," said Jennifer. "What can happen to work while it sits in an in-basket or e-mail inbox? Only two things can happen: *anything* and *everything*. This uncontrolled flow is subject to everything you mentioned and more. I think we'd all agree it does us no good for work to sit around waiting like this. Going forward, we're going to try to prevent this from happening, and continuous flow is how we're going to do it."

"OK," I said. "But how are we supposed to do this without getting rid of individual in-baskets or e-mail inboxes and combining them all? Not to mention, because each associate is a shared resource whose activities take different amounts of time to complete, they'd all be waiting around for one another to finish their work. Surely, we don't want to do that!"

"Let me reply to your two concerns," said Jennifer. "One is shared resources, and the other is different or varying task times. First, regarding shared resources, because people work on many different things throughout the day, full-time continuous flow usually isn't an option, so we use part-time continuous flow instead. We can colocate associates for regularly scheduled periods of time, during which we have them operate in continuous flow or process one, move one fashion. We call this group a *processing cell*, and we set it up to complete work based on an established takt time. When the processing cell meets, there are no priority changes or interruptions, and the work never waits." She went to the easel and drew a diagram of the idea (Figure 7.5).

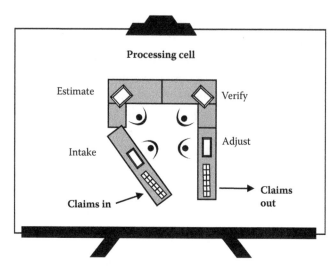

FIGURE 7.5

An example of a processing cell, where four employees complete work in a process one, move one fashion.

I nodded to Jennifer and gave her a look of partial satisfaction. I understood the part-time colocation idea, but I still doubted that Jennifer could get all the associates in the cell to do their work in the same amount of time.

"For this part-time cell to function properly, it needs to have all the equipment, tools, files, reference books, materials, and network access required to process the work, and we need to make sure everyone's work takes roughly the same amount of time to complete and is as close to the established takt time as possible," said Jennifer. "We don't want anyone in the cell waiting to receive work from the previous person or activity.

"Let me introduce another term called *work elements*. A work element is defined as the smallest, discrete increment of required work that can be moved to and completed by another person. They're logical breaking points in the sequence of tasks we do that make up the work as we know it: thinking, composing, editing, calculating, filing, communicating, documenting, retrieving, saving, and so on. We take everyone's discrete tasks that make up the total process, disassociate those tasks from specific individuals, and then redistribute them in sequence so each associate's total work takes slightly less time than the takt time established for the takt capability.

"So, we give the first associate in our processing cell enough work elements, in the correct sequence, of course, so that he or she produces at slightly less than the established takt time. We then take the remaining work elements and continue to redistribute them in sequence to the next associate in the processing cell until he or she also produces at slightly less than the established takt time. We continue until we're out of work elements." Jennifer sketched this for us on the flip chart (Figure 7.6).

"If the work elements for the last person in the cell fall further below the takt capability time, that's OK. They could bring in some extra work to help offset the time they would otherwise be idle. For everyone else, we want the work elements to add up to slightly less than the takt capability time, or at least as close as possible.

"I've oversimplified things here somewhat, and I recognize that we may bump up against some personal barriers when we do this, but that's a cultural issue. For right now, though, can you see how the work element concept can be used to redistribute work, create and maintain flow, and avoid having people sit around and wait?"

"You've certainly made a good argument for part-time continuous flow, and addressed the issues I had," I said. "But, I'll have to think about the specifics some more. In the meantime, what do you do with a work element that's tied to a person with a unique skill?"

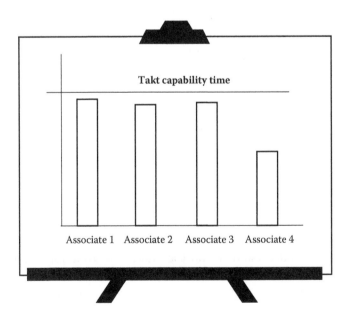

FIGURE 7.6
Work elements redistributed so each associate completes his/her work under the established takt capability time.

"Good question, Pat, and it tells me you're considering how you might apply this idea at your company," replied Jennifer. "When we go to implementation, we may need to do some cross-training if someone's skill set or knowledge prevents us from achieving continuous flow. Often, we need to consider which work elements are *core work* and which ones are *noncore work*. Core work can't be moved to someone else because it requires specialized training, whereas noncore work can be shifted around with a little training or education. For example, an engineer probably can't do an accountant's job, and vice versa, but they both could probably be trained to fill out header information for the other person.

"This might limit our ability to colocate people in part-time processing cells, but we'll still see benefits from bringing everyone together and eliminating wait times for the work. If someone's processing time is lower than everyone else's and there's nothing we can do about it, then they could bring other work to complete while they are idle, but the work being completed in the processing cell would need to be given priority all the time."

"It seems like the work elements can be reassigned to accommodate various takt times, but what happens when we actually find ourselves in a different takt capability?" asked Peyton. "It seems like a lot of work to reassign all those work elements every time the takt capability changes."

"Another great observation," said Jennifer. "We'll be talking about something called standard work in guideline number six, which will help us capture and define how we distribute the work elements for each takt capability. When the takt capability changes, the associates might meet more often, work longer hours, or add people to the processing cell. The standard work tells them what to do in each case, without management. The associates will simply reference the different, preestablished distributions in work elements. So, to answer your question, the different work element distributions have already been preestablished before they are ever needed or used.

"There are many options for designing your processing cell to meet different takt times. I won't get into the details now—I'll leave those for the reference books*—but it's possible to figure out how many associates you need for each takt capability and the amount of time for which they're needed."

"But none of this is really new," I said. "I saw something like this at my old company. One of the departments had a study hall period, during

---

* See the Bibliography at the end of this book.

which a group of associates would meet each day for a specific, uninterrupted period of time to complete their routine assignments. I'm not sure they took it to the level of takt capability or work element distribution, but the group had a good performance record."

"Well, I certainly don't know what happened at your old company, so I can't say what they did or didn't do," said Jennifer. "But based on my experience, I know that some companies do a great job creating isolated processing cells, or something we might call pockets of flow, very similar to what we just discussed. What they usually don't do, however, is *connect* these isolated cells to all the other activities that have to take place in the office to complete the work, and the work just piles up and waits somewhere else even longer than it did before because nothing is connected. This is a great segue into our next guideline."

FIFO (FIRST IN, FIRST OUT)

Jennifer continued on to the next topic without missing a beat. "Now, we may be able to create some part-time processing cells, but we're going to encounter situations that will prevent us from creating them everywhere, and that's OK. So, let's talk about what we can do when that happens.

"If we can't create processing cells everywhere, we're going to use a guideline called FIFO, which stands for first in, first out. Most people are familiar with this term from its use in accounting. For our purposes, though, we want to think of FIFO as a form of flow used to regulate the sequence and volume of work between two disconnected processes. This could be connecting a processing cell to the next activity or just connecting two activities, neither of which are processing cells.

"Let's do an exercise to help us understand how FIFO works. Say we introduce blue, green, yellow, and red ping-pong balls into the top end of a pipe. In what order do you think the balls would come out the other end of the pipe?"

"In the same order they went in," replied Peyton. "Blue, green, yellow, and red. That's a no-brainer."

"Good," said Jennifer. "Now, let's imagine that Pat is loading the pipe with a certain color ping-pong ball, and Peyton is unloading a ball from the pipe at a regular time interval. Pat, you have a large supply of colored ping-pong balls, but let's say the pipe is only long enough to hold five at a time. What's the lowest and highest number of ping-pong balls that could be in the pipe at any given time?"

"Zero and five," replied Peyton.

"Right again," said Jennifer. "Do you see how the length of the pipe controlled the amount of ping-pong balls that could go into it? It's very different from an in-basket or email inbox, where files stack up higher than the sides and any number of jobs might be present. In our exercise, Peyton, you were removing individual ping-pong balls from the pipe, but how did you decide which ping-pong ball to take when you were ready for the next one?"

Peyton seemed a bit puzzled. "I'm not sure what you're getting at. I wouldn't really have any choice. I would just take whichever ping-pong ball is next in line in the pipe. It's not like I could pull some out until I found a favorite color and then reload the extras back into the pipe, could I?"

"Perhaps the question was ambiguous, but I like your answer," said Jennifer. "You're right; you would simply withdraw the next one from the pipe."

She then went to the flip chart and constructed a diagram of two activities named Pat and Peyton and connected them with two parallel lines. Underneath the lines, she wrote "FIFO," and on top of them, she wrote "Max = 5 Balls." Then, she added balls of various colors (Figure 7.7).

"This diagram represents how we would connect two processes together using a FIFO lane," she said. "You'll see something like this when we take our tour this afternoon, but with jobs and work, not balls."

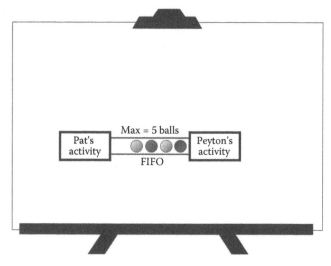

FIGURE 7.7
An example of two activities connected by FIFO.

She finished the drawing and turned back to us. "When the FIFO lane fills up, what happens to each of your activities?"

"Well, I wouldn't be able to put any more balls into the pipe," I said. "I'd have nothing to do."

"If you're a shared resource, you'd likely do something else for a while until an empty spot opens up in the FIFO lane," replied Jennifer. "You're correct, however, in assuming that if you continue to process work meant for Peyton's process, it would have nowhere to go. That would be a problem.

"If you can somehow help Peyton to get back on track, then that's great, but often this just isn't possible. A junior accountant might not be able to help the finance manager he's sending work to, but he could work on something else until space in the FIFO lane opens up again. This can get tricky, though. In the office, we would not want the process feeding the FIFO lane to stop sending its work. So, we would create an overflow FIFO lane, but as soon as it's used, it would be a signal to everyone that we're in an abnormal flow condition, and this would mean that some additional response is required.

"What about for you, Peyton? What would you do if the FIFO lane backs up?"

"I don't see any difference for me," said Peyton. "I would just keep doing what I normally do, but I imagine I'd be able to see when the FIFO lane becomes full, right?"

"That's right," said Jennifer. "We'll talk more about what we do in that situation when we get to the second part of our definition of Operational Excellence about fixing flow before it breaks down, although some of what I just mentioned will apply."

She turned back to the diagram and added another FIFO lane off to Peyton's right and connected it to a processing cell. It was clear from the example that the processing cell would always know what to work on next from the FIFO lane that fed it (Figure 7.8).

"For the moment, I want you to recall the five questions we asked previously to determine if we had flow," said Jennifer. "Peyton, do you want to try answering them again, this time using this example? Let's say it takes you 20 minutes to 'process' a ball from the FIFO lane once you withdraw it."

"OK," said Peyton. "I'll give it a try. The first question is, how do I know what to work on next? That's easy. I just take whatever is in the FIFO lane. The second question is, where do I get my work from? That one's simple, too. I get it from the FIFO lane, and I'm sure in a real one, there would be a specific spot from which I would retrieve my work or maybe even a

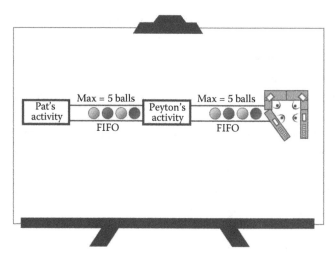

FIGURE 7.8

A processing cell connected by FIFO to the two previous activities.

specific folder in my e-mail inbox. The third question is, how long should it take to perform my work? You said 20 minutes, so that's how I know.

"The fourth question is, where do I send my work once I'm finished with it? I would put it in the FIFO lane that feeds the processing cell. Again, in a real-life setting, I'm sure there would be a specific spot in which I'd put completed work or maybe even a specific e-mail title to use so it could be funneled to a specific folder in someone else's e-mail inbox. The fifth question is, when I send my work, is flow still normal? The FIFO lane going to the processing cell determines this one. If there is an open space, then I know flow is normal. If the space isn't open, we have abnormal flow, and everyone would know an additional response is required."

"Nicely done," said Jennifer. "There might even be situations where we need to use multiple FIFO lanes if more than one type of work is flowing into the same processing cell. If we have multiple FIFO lanes, we need to have an indicator that tells us which FIFO lane to pull from next. The indicator could be an arrow or a sign that says 'Next Job' or 'Complete This Next.' No matter how many FIFO lanes we have, we should always be able to answer the five questions for flow for each one."

"That's why FIFO is considered a form of flow, isn't it?" I asked. "Because we're able to answer those five questions?"

"Exactly," said Jennifer. "Continuous flow and FIFO tell us how the work will flow, but what about *when* the work will flow? That brings us to the next guideline."

WORKFLOW CYCLES

"A *workflow cycle* refers to the rate at which work moves or flows within or between different work areas or departments along a fixed pathway," said Jennifer. "This guideline builds on what we already established with our other ones, and it adds structure and discipline to them, too.

"Workflow cycles help us stabilize and regulate flow in the office, and they enable everyone to know the time at which they're going to receive their work. It's not an expediting system, but rather an indicator that tells us when work is going to flow along preset pathways and when knowledge will be captured. To ensure consistent, predictable results, workflow cycles should occur at preset time intervals."

Jennifer walked back to the easel, then turned around. "Let me give you a specific example," she said. "In our FIFO exercise, let's look at just Peyton's activity and the processing cell now. We would define a workflow cycle that describes the time at which the cell will process work and for how long it needs to process work. We might design it so the cell processes work every day for 2 hours, beginning at 1 o'clock." Jennifer drew on the flip chart, adding more information to a portion of the previous FIFO example (Figure 7.9).

"We want to create a workflow cycle at this level whether we're dealing with an activity done by only one associate or a processing cell staffed with multiple associates. Somewhere in the area, we want to indicate to

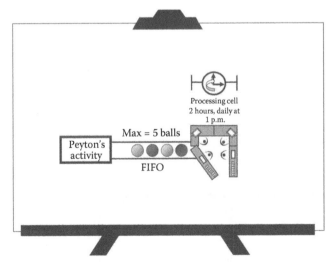

FIGURE 7.9
A workflow cycle created for the processing cell.

everyone that the associates in the cell have essentially promised to process everything in the FIFO lane by a certain time each day."

"So, this helps the associates know when to expect output from a particular activity or processing cell?" I asked.

"Yes," said Jennifer. "Because work flows at the processing cell at a preset time and along a preset pathway, everyone knows when they should expect to get their work from it, but that's not all. There are different levels of workflow cycles, too. The concept applies between multiple activities and processing cells from the start of the flow to the end. If everything in the office operates to a workflow cycle, then we're able to establish a *guaranteed turnaround time* for the entire office. This means that the time by which work will be completed is repeatable, predictable, and known in advance by everyone in the company."

She added even more detail to the example (Figure 7.10). "We can do this because we know how long it takes for work to be completed at each individual step, and we also know when work will be passed along to the next activity through the FIFO lane. If we know these two elements at every step in our office, then we know the guaranteed turnaround time for the entire office. Think of the advantage you would have over your competitors if you could provide guaranteed turnaround times to your customers."

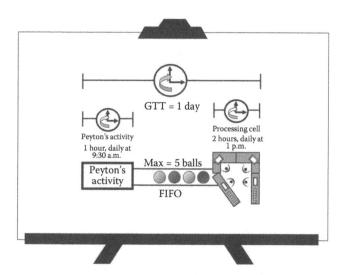

FIGURE 7.10

A workflow cycle created for the first process and another, overarching workflow cycle created for the entire end-to-end flow, which establishes a guaranteed turnaround time (GTT) for that flow.

"It makes sense," said Peyton. "No wonder this system is being introduced to other areas here. It not only creates flow, but also establishes guaranteed turnaround times for our work that we can share internally and with our clients."

"You got it," said Jennifer. "Having workflow cycles eliminates the need for countless voice mails and e-mails because people know when they'll receive their information. Each area in the office knows when a claim will be finished, so they don't need to check on it."

"The workflow cycle concept isn't as confusing as I first thought," I said. "But, what about if we have office processes that don't happen very often, like closing out the books for a quarter?"

"Great question," said Jennifer. "In that case, we would use something called an integration event, which is the fifth guideline."

INTEGRATION EVENTS

"Integration events* are a formal handoff of information between different areas of the office," said Jennifer. "They pull large amounts of information forward from one area to another by matching the output of the parties providing the information with the inputs required by the party receiving the information to ensure information flows and knowledge is captured."

"So, we might use an integration event to close out the books, like Pat mentioned," said Peyton.

"Yes," said Jennifer. "Another example could be turning over a project for executive approval. The vice president receiving the project package would need to be given all the information required to sign off on it, without having to go back and track down anything missing. The departments providing the information would make sure that their output matches with the inputs required by the vice president." She drew a quick picture on the flip chart (Figure 7.11).

"That seems to happen every now and then where I am," said Pat. "The information gets where it needs to go eventually, but not without a good amount of rework and arm twisting; sometimes, it can get even worse."

---

* Integration events were first used in product development (Kennedy 2003).

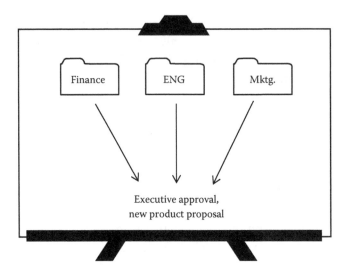

FIGURE 7.11
During the integration event, each department (Finance, Engineering, and Marketing) provides the outputs necessary to match the inputs that are needed by the executive in order to create a new product proposal.

"You've actually hit on one of the key elements of integration events," said Jennifer. "They are strictly the transfer of large amounts of information from one area of the business to another. It's not a milestone meeting. There's no bargaining, cajoling, negotiating, or asking questions, and no decisions should be made. All the information that's needed is provided in the format in which it's needed. This way, the person receiving the work can do what they need to do with it without any additional processing."

"That sounds like it would be a good way to determine if one department hasn't been able to keep up," I said. "If everyone is supposed to deliver their information at one preset time, then it would be easy to see who hasn't."

"That's true," said Jennifer. "Integration events shouldn't be meetings or status checkups, but they would provide visibility into this like you're saying."

"So, to make this work, there need to be standardized procedures for the flow, right?"

"I think you're hinting at standard work, Pat," said Jennifer. "Let's talk about that now. It's the next guideline. We need to develop robust standard work to establish regularity and consistency in our activities, part-time processing cells, and FIFO lanes. When we do, we'll hit our workflow cycles and guaranteed turnaround times every time."

STANDARD WORK

"The sixth guideline is critical to the successful operation of our office," said Jennifer. "Standard work means establishing the one best way to do a job or task and then ensuring everyone uses that method so that the work required is performed the same way and in a consistent amount of time, every time. Standard work helps us create a disciplined plan that all associates can follow, and we won't just have standard work for how we do things in the office. We'll also have standard work for the flow.

"In our office, we need to develop standard work for the flow of knowledge and information, and flow cannot exist without stability and repeatability in the things we do. Processing cells, FIFO, and workflow cycles provide the pathway and timing for flow, and standard work helps make the pathways and connections robust and keeps work moving along the connections we set up.

"It's not always easy to create or sustain standard work in the office, though. Education and leadership are critical, and so is a destination so people understand exactly what standard work should look like once it's achieved. Management needs to prepare the organization first and then drive the process and methodology for creating standard work.

"Is there a go-to person in your office who knows how to get things done? In most organizations, a lot of activities happen only because of the longevity of the workforce, or something we call tribal knowledge. Different individuals informally create work standards that they use to complete their work correctly. But, the details generally aren't documented, and the knowledge resides only with a few people, which means it has the potential to be discarded when people take vacation, are relocated, or retire.

"Standard work captures the best practices and lessons learned from each associate. Having the work defined and documented makes training more effective for new or temporary employees. A consistent approach and methodology also minimize the chance of introducing noise or chaos into the system. Things are done correctly, consistently, and with less variation from person to person because everyone uses the same method. In essence, standard work leads to better quality, lower cost, and improved morale."

I got the feeling Jennifer had lots of experience discussing this topic, as she seemed to speak with authority, wisdom, and as someone who had fought this battle many times before.

"People generally learn in three different ways," she said. "By hearing, seeing, and doing. We retain less than 5% of the information we hear when we're learning something new. When we see it, we retain about 60%. But, when we learn by doing, we retain approximately 90% of the information because we trust what we do. Standard work makes use of the best methods of learning by allowing associates to participate in the learning. They hear it explained, watch the process, and then perform the task using standard work to guide them. What method have we been using this morning?"

"Mostly hearing," said Peyton. "There's been a little watching, because of your drawings, and some doing with the exercises, so I guess we can't be expected to remember much by tomorrow."

That frightened me. I had heard a lot of good stuff so far, and to think I might not be able to put it all together for Chris was disturbing.

"That's right, and that's why we're rushing through this morning," said Jennifer. "Before the memories fade, I want you to take the tour and see what you've heard. Peyton, you'll have the opportunity to actually *do* all of this in the near future. Pat, I hope the 60% retention rate will work for you if you lean on your experience.

"All right, back to standard work. Once we develop standard work, we should always use it because it represents the best method for how to do things. If you stop and think about it, why would we ever use anything else? Once we create standard work, we need to recognize that it can be improved at any time. However, it's difficult to improve results if we only rely on one person or a select few, especially if one of them is the boss. If you're looking for ways to improve existing standard work, make sure you involve everyone."

Shifting gears, Jennifer suggested we jot down the next part.

"In Operational Excellence, there are two levels of standard work: activity level and flow level. Be sure to keep the levels separate rather than trying to combine them." She started on a new page on the flip chart and wrote down the two levels (Figure 7.12). "Both of these represent a level at which we need standard work," said Jennifer. "I'll explain each level and what the differences are between them.

"Activity-level standard work occurs at the level of an individual. Here, we want to describe what the job is, who is responsible for doing it—titles, not people's names—and how long they should work on it. We also want to include the content, tools, systems needed, sequence required for completing the work, and any other necessary information. This makes for

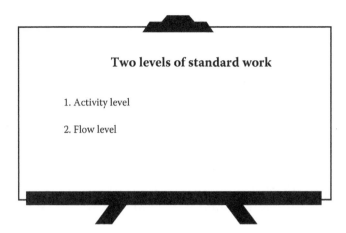

FIGURE 7.12
The two levels of standard work: the activity level and the flow level.

a better and more optimized process. Any questions about activity-level standard work?"

I felt an obligation to ask, given the opportunity. "So, activity-level standard work just details what an associate does for the job, things like the file used, the references, the specifics about documenting or creating a claim entry. This is where I might use photos, diagrams, screenshots—stuff like that, right?"

"That's correct," replied Jennifer. "It doesn't need to be complicated. In fact, the simpler the better. Also, remember that whatever you create will likely be improved regularly, so structure your documentation to allow for that and, as a leader, encourage it.

"Let's look at the flow level next. This is where we connect the activity of one person to the activity of another. This level of standard work answers questions such as, How do I know what to work on next? How and when do I pass work to the next process? What are the connections between activities? These are all flow-level questions, and they involve team activities and multiple people. Any questions here?"

"So, this is where the rules for FIFO and workflow cycles would come into play?" asked Peyton.

"Yes, exactly," said Jennifer. "Certain parts of flow-level standard work will already be settled by virtue of the rules of FIFO and workflow cycles, but it's also where our five questions for flow come into play. If we have good flow-level standard work, then we should be able to answer all five questions for each connection in our office."

Jennifer flipped back to the easel page with the five questions for flow (Figure 7.13). "Flow-level standard work establishes the standard for normal flow between activities," said Jennifer. "If employees can see normal flow, then they can see abnormal flow, which I'll talk more about later."

With the morning slipping away, and apparently much more to cover, Jennifer's pace picked up noticeably.

"All of the guidelines we've covered so far, as well as the ones we haven't, tie together," she said. "It's difficult to separate them when they build on one another in an integrated system. The first six guidelines we covered—takt and takt capability, continuous flow, FIFO, workflow cycles, integration events, and standard work—all make up how we design our flow. The next three guidelines we're going to cover will describe how we operate it on a day-to-day basis.

"Let's take a short break and arrange for lunch. We'll be ordering from the deli in our cafeteria, so here's a menu for each of you. Just check off what you want, and it'll be delivered so we can continue our conversation while we eat. Sorry to take that hour away from you, but we're packing a lot into one day."

Jennifer collected our forms and handed them to someone who was responsible for making sure our orders got to the right place at the right time. While we waited for our lunches, I reviewed my notes, eager to see what would come next.

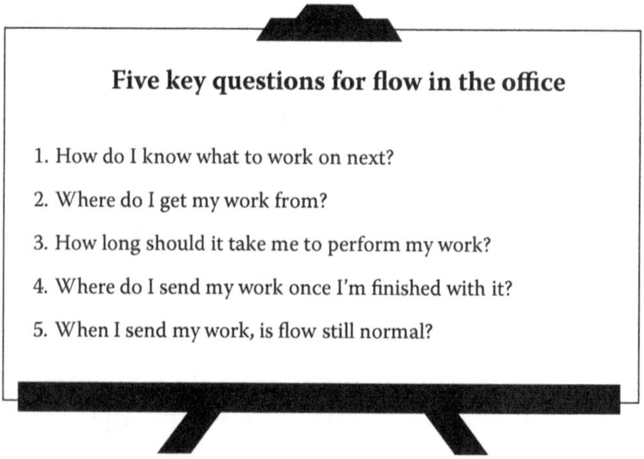

Five key questions for flow in the office

1. How do I know what to work on next?

2. Where do I get my work from?

3. How long should it take me to perform my work?

4. Where do I send my work once I'm finished with it?

5. When I send my work, is flow still normal?

FIGURE 7.13
The five key questions for flow in the office.

FROM THE AUTHOR

The first six guidelines constitute the design of flow for the office. Starting with takt and takt capability and working through activity- and flow-level standard work, each guideline builds on the last and creates the operational design for how information will flow and knowledge will be captured in the office.

With the first six guidelines in place, we should be able to answer the five questions for flow at each activity by establishing formal connections between them. These five questions tell us how and when work will be completed at each activity and how and when it will move to the next activity. By following these design guidelines, everyone in the office knows how and when information will flow. All of the e-mails and phone calls that are generated to find information are eliminated, and with this, the office environment becomes more stable.

In addition to bringing stability to the office, the first six guidelines begin to create the ability to distinguish between normal and abnormal flow. Establishing a takt capability, for example, lets everyone know the volume and mix of work that can be processed within a given amount of time. If customer requests exceed either of these established parameters (or both), then everyone immediately knows and understands that the office is in an abnormal condition.

Continuous flow and FIFO help distinguish between normal and abnormal flow also, as both have specific rules that govern their operation. Work is not allowed to pile up between activities in a processing cell, and each FIFO lane has a "max" associated with it. If we find that work *is* piling up in a processing cell, or that FIFO lanes have exceeded their max, then everyone quickly and easily can see that something has gone wrong.

While continuous flow and FIFO establish normality and abnormality for the *quantity* of work permitted, workflow cycles do it for the *timing*. With workflow cycles created at each activity or processing cell in the flow, everyone will know the time by which work should be completed. From this knowledge, the timing of the end-to-end flow can be determined and a guaranteed turnaround time established for all customer requests.

The first six guidelines create a powerful design for flow in the office, and combining them with the final three guidelines sets organizations on the right path to achieve Operational Excellence in their offices.

8

The Education, Part II

After the break, Jennifer pulled us together for a quick review before moving on. "Let's do a recap of the first six guidelines," she said. "Who wants to tell me what they are?"

"The first guideline is takt and takt capability," I said. "First, we look at our demand profile and determine how many takt capabilities we need. Then, for each takt capability, we determine a takt time, and this is the rate at which we need to complete work for a service our office provides."

Peyton jumped in and said, "The second guideline is continuous flow, where we analyze all the activities, colocate associates, balance work elements, and design a part-time processing cell that operates on a process one, move one basis. Because we set up this cell with the ability to flex to different takt capabilities as well as meet at regular, preset times, we always know when information will flow, and we're able to remove a lot of the waiting that plagues the office.

"The third guideline is first in, first out, or FIFO, which is a form of flow used to regulate the sequence and volume of work between two disconnected or imbalanced activities. FIFO allows us to keep work in sequence between activities if we're not using continuous flow. It also creates robust connections between activities in the office."

"The fourth guideline is workflow cycles," I said. "We use them to establish preset pathways and timing for the flow of information between activities and connections throughout the entire office. With robust workflow cycles, we're able to flow work through our office at guaranteed turnaround times.

"The fifth guideline is integration events, which are formal handoffs that pull large amounts of information forward from one area of the office to another by matching the outputs of the parties providing the information with the inputs required by the party receiving it. They're not milestone meetings, and no decisions should be made at them.

"The sixth guideline is standard work, which helps establish regularity and consistency at our activities, continuous flow processing cells, and FIFO lanes. Standard work is applied at the activity level to tell us how a process should function and at the flow level to link different activities and processing cells together. Standard work enables us to consistently hit our workflow cycles and predictably flow work through the office at guaranteed turnaround times."

"Wow," said Jennifer. "You both pass with flying colors."

"So, are we done now?" I asked.

"Not yet," she said Jennifer. "Remember, the first six guidelines were all about how we design our office for flow. The remaining ones we're going to cover are about how we operate that flow. Let's get started on the last three."

SINGLE-POINT INITIALIZATION

"Now, we want to address how we initialize work into the flow and maintain a set sequence until the request is delivered to the customer. When an assignment is started in a typical business process, each associate sets his or her own priorities and then pushes completed work to the next step, *whether it needs it or not.* This approach provides no regularity or predictability to the flow of work in the office, and it causes us to meddle and shift priorities around.

Using the first six guidelines, we've designed an office where each activity is linked or connected in flow all the way to the customer."

Jennifer walked to the easel and added a person at the end of the diagram she had drawn previously (Figure 8.1). "Here's our customer, all the way on the right," she said, pointing at the stick figure. "And on the left are the activities and connections that deliver our work to that customer. But, where and how does the work get started? If it's possible, we want to have only one place at which we initialize the flow, and we call this the *initialization point.*

"All of our office flow happens *after* the point at which we initialize the work. From there, we process in continuous flow or FIFO all the way to the customer. This is an important point because if the sequence of work

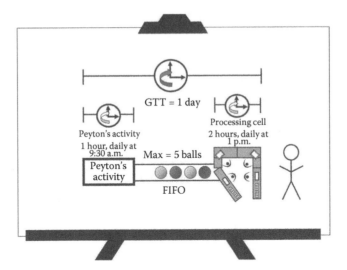

FIGURE 8.1
The customer receives the completed work from this flow.

remains fixed after the initialization point, and if we know how long each step takes, then we can predict the time it'll take for work to be completed once it's been released into our system. That's how we're able to create and live by those guaranteed turnaround times we've been talking about."

"So, we introduce a job at the initialization point and, after that, we have flow all the way to the customer so the sequence of work remains fixed," said Peyton.

"Yes," said Jennifer. "However, it might be necessary to resequence work at fixed points in the flow because of external factors beyond our control. For example, if work has to go to an outside entity halfway through the flow, be reviewed, and then reenter the flow, the reentry point could be a good spot to resequence the work, if it's necessary. This would be called a *sequencing point*. These sequencing points need to be well defined if they exist and shouldn't be based on management priorities but rather external factors."

Jennifer turned to a new page on the flip chart and drew another diagram (Figure 8.2). "In this example, the initialization point is the first process. After 'Estimate,' work moves in FIFO through the rest of the flow, but once the estimator is finished, work goes out for 'Customer Review,' which is outside the office. Because we can't control when or the order in which the customer will send completed work back to us, the process that receives

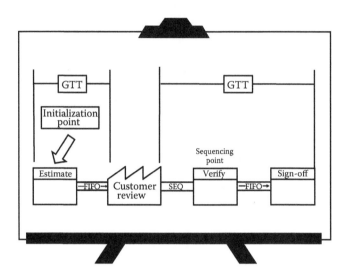

FIGURE 8.2

Separate GTTs exist for the segments of flow that occur before and after "Customer Review," the external factor that causes the need for a sequencing point at "Verify" as work comes back into the office.

the work from the customer can be a sequencing point. Remember we use sequencing points only when outside factors beyond our control warrant them, like customers needing to review work midway through the flow, not because of management priorities.

"At 'Verify,' work can be resequenced as it comes back into the flow from the customer, then this sequence would carry through the rest of the flow. All the work that happens before and after 'Customer Review' is within our span of control, so we can create two separate guaranteed turnaround times: one governing everything that happens before the work goes out to the customer and the other governing everything that happens when the work returns from the customer. Note that if we have a sequencing point in the flow, we put 'SEQ' in the lane instead of 'FIFO' so everyone knows that the process being fed by the lane is a sequencing point."

"So, the initialization point helps create a guaranteed turnaround time for the entire flow and allows us to predict the time by which we'll complete the work," said Peyton. "If there's an external process involved, like the 'Customer Review' step in your diagram, we can create a sequencing point where the work returns to the flow and set guaranteed turnaround times for what we're able to control before and after the external portion. Just to be clear, you're talking about the same work that's in my department right now, all those jobs that have unknown completion dates?"

"Yes," said Jennifer. "Sound believable?"

"Not really," I replied. "I admit you've constructed a good case for designing flow to improve performance, but you're telling us that we can launch a job into the office, never change priorities, and be certain of its completion time! I've got to see it to believe it."

"Well, later today, you'll get to see it happen," said Jennifer. "I remember how astonished I was when I saw it in action the first time. The tour this afternoon should be like a walk through an amusement park for you. But right now, I want to make sure the concept at least makes sense."

"It does," I said. "I'm just not sure how to make it happen."

"Fair enough," said Jennifer. "Let's get back to our discussion so we'll have time for the tour. In our diagram, is there one point at which we could initialize the work that would enable every other activity to know what to do next?"

Not getting a response right away, she went on. "Let's look to the left of the customer. We have a processing cell operating on a workflow cycle of 2 hours each day. The jobs come to it from the FIFO lane and are then processed. The processing cell always knows what to do next because the FIFO lane maintains the sequence of work that comes from Peyton's activity."

She drew a circle around the box at the left and put an arrow over it (Figure 8.3). "Peyton's activity is the only one that needs to be scheduled

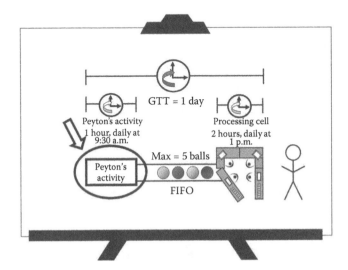

FIGURE 8.3
Work is initialized at only one process or activity in the flow, usually as far upstream as possible.

because the processing cell will know what to work on next based on what comes to it in the FIFO lane. So, Peyton's activity is where we would initialize the work."

Jennifer pointed at Peyton's activity and said, "This is the first activity. How does Peyton know what to do? Well, Peyton's work comes in from the customer. In this example, the customer requests a ball, so Peyton processes the ball and then puts it into the FIFO lane. After that, we have either continuous flow or FIFO all the way to the customer, so the sequence of work never changes.

"The reason we aim for door-to-door flow in our business processes is so the work goes out in the same order it comes in. Once we introduce work at the initialization point, the sequence never changes, and this establishes a guaranteed turnaround time for the entire office.

"It's important to become aware of problems at the initialization point because this is the first place, and sometimes the only place, where work is sequenced for every other activity and processing cell in the office. If we have issues there, then we'll end up with irregular flow, and that's when managers tend to want to jump in."

"It seems that our initialization point might have a bit of uncertainty around it if we need to follow up on certain customer requests or clarify information," I said. "Also, priorities can be adjusted at this point before work is released into the flow. Is that accurate?"

"Yes," answered Jennifer. "But it's limited to this one process in the flow. If a customer request isn't sufficiently complete to process when we receive it, unfortunately, we can't release it into the flow. We would need to clarify information or request missing data, and we would need to develop standard work to do it. Even though there might be some uncertainty at the initialization point, after that, we've essentially eliminated the chaos that used to exist because it all takes place up front now. We also want to put standard work around how the sequence is determined at the initialization point so the same sequence will be generated no matter who is handling the process. Does that answer your question?"

"Yes," I said. "But what about setting priorities at the initialization point?"

"Ah, I see what you mean," said Jennifer. "Having a robust initialization point allows the business to rearrange work any way it wants *before* fixing the sequence and introducing it into the flow. If certain types of work are more important than others, maybe because of the customer or the amount of work involved, then this is a good place to sequence the work to account for these realities while still ensuring the sequence can be preserved through the entirety of the flow. Is that a more comprehensive answer?"

"Yes," I said. "It's a lot to digest, but I understand the concepts."

"Also, keep in mind that although we move all the clarification up front to this one process, it's still a waste of time," said Jennifer. "If we can minimize clarification, then we should. But, removing all the uncertainty and reprioritization from the activities that come *after* the initialization point is what allows us to establish a guaranteed turnaround time for the office.

"If we set priorities at the initialization point, sequence jobs there, and have flow all the way after it, would there ever be a need for prioritization? Why or why not?"

"Once a job is in flow, we don't need to shuffle anything around since the desired sequence of work has already been established and is preserved all the way to the customer," said Peyton. "Since every job has a guaranteed turnaround time associated with it, we'll always know when a job should be complete. Each job is already being done as quickly as possible, so why would we want to interfere with that? Unless it's due to outside factors, then we can use the sequencing point concept you described previously.

"Otherwise, I'd probably just check to make sure we were using the correct takt capability and verify that our standard work is correct. It seems like it would make more sense to critique the system rather than expedite a specific job, which would ignore the underlying problem."

"But, what happens when the information on a claim finally comes through and now it's a rush because it's so far behind?" I asked. "Surely, we're not just going to let it wait in line behind all the others."

"Unexpected things will always happen," said Jennifer. "We can't predict everything, but we're always going to try to let the system handle anything that comes up because it's designed to be flexible. For example, if a claim is in rush status, we could run our workflow cycles more frequently or perhaps start them a few hours earlier. The point is that we're going to look to the *system* when something unexpected happens, *not* to the decisions of managers."

"OK, that makes sense," I said.

"Then I think we're ready to shift gears," said Jennifer. "Until now, we've been talking about the first part of the definition of Operational Excellence. Who can remind me what that is?"

I spoke up and said, "Where we see the flow of value to the customer."

"That's right," said Jennifer. "Everything we've covered has been necessary for us to see the flow of value to the customer, but let me ask you this. Why are we creating flow in the first place? What's so good about flow?"

Peyton and I sat quietly for what seemed like a few minutes before I answered.

"Well, creating flow is the best way to eliminate waste."

I was confident in what I'd said, but I got the sense that Jennifer was after something deeper.

"This is a tricky one," she said. "Although it's true that creating flow is the best way to eliminate waste, the real reason we create flow is *simply so we can see when flow stops*. If flow has stopped, then we know something has gone wrong, and we can step in, fix it, and get the flow back on track. Actually, you and I won't step in. The employees will, and this gets us into the second part of the definition of Operational Excellence, fixing flow before it breaks down. The next two guidelines explain how to create a system that lets us know if things are going right or wrong and how we can set up our employees to fix flow before it breaks down."

━━━━━━━━━━

PITCH

Jennifer continued: "Next, we'll look at something called pitch, which is used for two purposes. First, it lets the people in the flow see if things are going right or starting to go wrong, and second, it enables everyone else to know if information will get to the next activity, processing cell, or FIFO lane on time.

"Now that we understand the way knowledge and information flow in our office and how and why they are initiated at only one point, let's talk about how we can see if things are going right or wrong, and how often we should do so. Do you think we can we see how well things are going in today's offices?"

"Is that a rhetorical question?" asked Peyton. "Because to me, the answer is, not really. Any checks by management happen in meetings or are totally random, kind of like a surprise audit. But, in their defense, they have no way of knowing if everyone is completing their jobs on time unless they stand over their shoulders and watch them work."

"Sometimes, that kind of micromanagement is what drives changes in priorities," I added. "That, and not knowing when the work will be completed."

Jennifer knew she struck a chord with her question. "Your responses are spot on. Let's think about how often we should know if our system is keeping up with customer demand. Should a manager know every Friday so he or she can prepare an end-of-week report? Probably not, because if customer demand has changed during the week or things have fallen behind somewhere, then there wouldn't be enough time left to do anything about it."

Peyton and I nodded in agreement. "I'd want to know there's a problem as soon as one arises," I said.

"Fair enough," said Jennifer. "But, how would you actually go about doing this? Would you walk through the office every hour to see what's on time and what's behind by asking each associate how it's going? If you took this approach, how much time would you spend at your desk getting your own work done? What signs would you look for when strolling around that would tip you off to a problem?"

"I'm not sure," I said. "I'd know a problem if I saw one, though, but I guess I probably *would* spend a lot of time asking questions and trying to fix things."

"You're exactly right," said Jennifer. "I don't want *you* fixing anything. We want to use pitch to tell everyone when things are going right or starting to go wrong. We also want to establish a predetermined time at which we know our system is keeping up with the rate of customer demand. Pitch gives everyone a true sense of the pulse of the office and also a feeling of accomplishment.

"A good pitch would be moving work from one activity or processing cell at a preset time and delivering it to the next process in the flow. Either the work moved at the preset time or it didn't. If it didn't, then everyone knows something is wrong. Because this can be tough to do in the office sometimes, we can even put up a signal like a flag to indicate if the flow is on time or behind. A green flag would mean everything is normal, while a red flag would mean something has gone wrong.

"To be clear, this is not about how often a manager or supervisor checks on the associates working in his or her area. Rather, it's about how often the associates know whether the flow is working the way it's supposed to. Pitch measures the *system*, not the people operating it."

Jennifer gave us time to grasp what she said, then continued. "Pitch is not always easy to create, but it should have four important attributes. Pitch should be visual, physical, binary, and anticipated." She went over to the easel and wrote these attributes down (Figure 8.4).

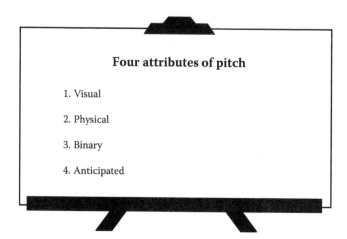

FIGURE 8.4
The four attributes of pitch.

"Let me explain a bit more. By visual, I mean we should be able to see whether we're on time without asking anyone. By physical, I mean some activity must happen, like a file is moved, a tray is emptied, a flag is raised, and so on. The best physical activity is actually moving work from one process to the next, but this is hard to do sometimes. By binary, I mean the flow happened or it did not, and by anticipated, I mean that we should know when the pitch is going to happen before it does, every time.

"So, how often should we know if the system is meeting customer demand?"

"Beats me, but I'm sure you'll be able to clear it up," I said.

"Thanks for your confidence," said Jennifer. "Like we agreed before, knowing at the end of every week is too infrequent. How about the other end of the spectrum? Imagine if our office processes worked really fast, let's say 3 minutes per job. Would we want to know every 3 minutes if the system was working?"

"No way," I said.

"Why not?" pressed Jennifer.

"Because if something went wrong, there wouldn't be enough time to do anything about it. There's no way anyone could react and fix things inside a 3-minute window. Plus, my associates would get sick of me if I wanted to know about their progress every 3 minutes."

"Very good," said Jennifer. "Depending on what you do in your office and how long your jobs take, the time increment used can vary. Generally, though, a good time increment for pitch is at the end of a workflow cycle, specifically, when a processing cell has finished."

She went to the easel and added more detail to the previous example (Figure 8.5). "The figure carrying the balls would be the person moving information to the next processing cell, activity, or even FIFO lane," said Jennifer. "Don't worry about the number of balls. In real life, this person would move the amount of work that was completed at the end of each workflow cycle. The clock above him means this happens at preset times. Just like the illustration, this can and probably will happen at different times for different processes. The flag system could be used here, too, to indicate if the flow is on time or behind.

"Don't worry if you miss your time target in the beginning. In fact, you likely will until the associates become comfortable with the new way of doing things. Remember that pitch is a check on the system, not the people operating it. Make sure your people understand this; otherwise, it can be pretty discouraging if the time target is repeatedly missed. Notice that I didn't say when the *associates* miss the time target. The success of pitch depends not only on how you deal with the technicalities involved, but also on how you introduce it to your people and how they understand it.

"What really counts, though, is what the people in the flow do when they see it's starting to break down, because that means something has gone

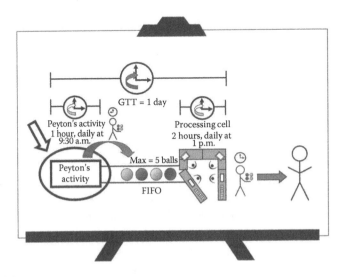

FIGURE 8.5

Pitch could be created at the end of "Peyton's Activity" and at the conclusion of the processing cell.

wrong and needs to be fixed. What we do about it and how we handle it brings us to our next and last guideline."

At that point, our lunches arrived, so we took a few minutes to get the food unwrapped and agreed to continue our discussion as we ate.

CHANGES IN DEMAND

"We've gone through eight guidelines so far," said Jennifer. "We've established multiple takt capabilities and created continuous flow processing cells, FIFO, workflow cycles, integration events, standard work, single-point initialization, and pitch. We've even been able to set up a guaranteed turnaround time for the entire flow through the office. What more could we need?"

Jennifer paused, expecting Peyton and I to pick up the conversation from there, and Peyton took the hint and gave Jennifer a chance to get started on her lunch.

"Well, what about if we end up routinely exceeding our takt capability?"

"Great point," I said. "But how exactly would we *know* we've exceeded our takt capability?"

"Our ninth guideline is something called changes in demand or, perhaps better put, *reacting* to changes in demand," said Jennifer. "It's going to really get into the second part of the definition of Operational Excellence: Fixing flow before it breaks down.

"First, we need to be able to react to the normal variation we experience on a day-to-day basis. This will be done through the FIFO lanes and work-flow cycles we create. They will be flexible enough to absorb a temporary increase in demand. But, we have to recognize when the actual demand has increased on a more permanent basis, which is something we expect to happen as we strive for Operational Excellence. As we begin to regularly meet or exceed our customers' expectations, it's possible—and even likely—that they'll reward us with more business, especially if we can outperform the competition. Operational Excellence is a foundation for business growth, and if we achieve it, our business will grow. But, more on that later.

"Right now, we want to address how we recognize and respond to changing customer demand. First, we need to understand what we normally deal with to know whether it's becoming or has become permanently abnormal. Let's look at a graph."

Jennifer handed us both a sheet of paper (Figure 8.6). "This is the actual demand we experienced 4 months ago. Note that the biggest demand days were every fifth day, or every Friday. As I mentioned, we determined that some of these peaks were self-imposed because one of our customer service associates was clearing his desk of any procrastinated work at the end of each week. This variation caused the demand to hit us in abnormal and irregular waves.

"We were able to eliminate this internally caused variation, but as you can see from the graph, we still had variation that we couldn't get rid of. So, what do we do? How do we staff for something like this when we have persistent variation?"

"No clue," I said. "I have this problem all the time, and I don't handle it very well."

"Let me help you out," said Jennifer. "Earlier, when we were talking about takt capabilities, I mentioned that we need to establish multiple takt capabilities to account for specific ranges of customer demand. Then, we create different takt capabilities to handle the different ranges in demand we expect to experience over the course of time."

Jennifer went to the easel and drew something that looked like a time card rack. She added folders in each slot and indicated that the slots would be colored differently (Figure 8.7). She continued: "This acts as a FIFO lane for work, and the colors tell us if demand is what we expected or if it has increased beyond the established takt capability. If work is only in the green areas, then we know demand is normal. If it's in the red, then we

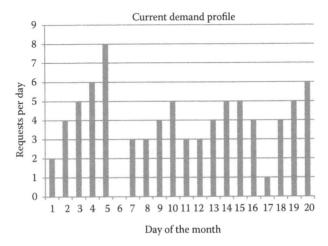

FIGURE 8.6
Demand over the course of a month, typically peaking every week on Friday.

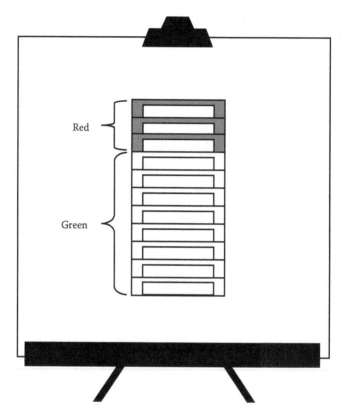

FIGURE 8.7
A color-coded setup that can be used to see changes in demand visually.

know demand is abnormal. If demand is in the red for a day or two, the team can make adjustments to how work flows through the office to keep up. Maybe they run a workflow cycle a little longer for those 2 days, but whatever standard work they use, it's only temporary to handle a short-term spike. All of this has been preestablished so it's ready to go before the associates even begin working for the day."

"OK," said Peyton. "So we know how we're going to handle daily changes in demand that are temporary, but what if we're in the red zone constantly and can't ever get out of it?"

"That can happen," said Jennifer. "When it does, we need to switch to another takt capability to handle the increased demand. There needs to be standard work for how to do this so the higher takt capability can be automatically deployed when needed. It might involve setting up parallel FIFO lanes or processing cells, creating new times for when the workflow cycles will run, creating a new pitch and, most important, new standard work for how the flow will operate to handle the increase in demand. It should be like flipping a switch, and everyone should know what to do once the switch is flipped because the response is preestablished.

"Having standard work for different takt capabilities gets to the heart of the second part of the definition of Operational Excellence: fixing flow before it breaks down. With this methodology in place, the associates can see flow breaking down and determine if the current takt capability is sufficient using the existing FIFO lanes and workflow cycles or if a more permanent alteration is needed. And, in case you haven't guessed by now, this all happens without management intervention of any kind.

"Think of what would happen if we didn't have standard work for when things go wrong. Typically, managers would become involved and change priorities, authorize overtime, or maybe just allow the jobs to be late. They'd make decisions, and *decisions kill flow*, but no more. Now, the associates can see that conditions are becoming abnormal, react to those signals, and fix the flow before it breaks down and negatively impacts the customer."

"So, the system flexes to accommodate the daily variation we experience, and can even signal when we need to tap into our standard work for when things go wrong," I said. "The associates, not the managers, are able to react to these changes and fix the flow before it breaks down. If we are in an abnormal state for more than a couple of days, then we know something else is going on and we need to switch takt capabilities. Is that right?"

Jennifer nodded, then continued. "All right, then. Before we go on the tour, keep in mind that I haven't told you everything today. There are more concepts that help us in the office, things like *knowledge shares*, which have virtually eliminated meetings for us. By meetings, I mean when we bring people together and then try to influence, cajole, and arm twist to make decisions. Perhaps we can talk about knowledge shares the next time you come visit us.

"If there are no questions, we're going to go on that tour I've been promising. While we're out in the office and meeting with the team, feel free to ask questions. The associates you'll be meeting haven't rehearsed for this, so you should get nothing but honest answers. Are you ready?"

We both answered in the affirmative and followed Jennifer out of the conference room and into her world of Operational Excellence.

FROM THE AUTHOR

The first six guidelines constitute the design of flow in the office and the final three describe how the flow will operate day in and day out. Together, they ensure that the office meets the established guaranteed turnaround time for the requested service. Because the last three guidelines detail the operation of the flow, they hold significant influence in achieving the guaranteed turnaround time.

Single-point initialization eliminates the tendency to reprioritize work once it enters the flow. If work must leave and come back, sequencing points are used. Pitch enables everyone to know if the flow is on time without asking questions or checking in throughout the day. Changes in demand create the ability to physically see if there is a need to switch to another takt capability and then do so, all without meetings or management intervention.

While the final three guidelines can have the greatest impact on the business, they can also be among the most challenging to implement, as they run counter to many traditional ways of working in the office. In most offices, the ability to reprioritize is central to management's sphere of authority, as the flexibility it provides is intended to enable quick reaction. Similarly, status updates are meant to monitor the office to check each day that orders will go out and jobs will be completed. If that is not happening, then it is management's responsibility to step in and do something about it.

With single-point initialization, pitch, and changes in demand in place, management intervention will rarely be needed, as the last three guidelines eliminate most of the causes that drive these practices in the first place. There will still be *some* management intervention in an office that has achieved Operational Excellence, as it is impossible to preplan for everything that might happen, but its occurrence will be greatly reduced.

While each guideline is important in and of itself, it is only together that they can provide a system of autonomous flow. No one guideline can individually reduce or eliminate management intervention in the day-to-day operation of the office, but together, and especially by implementing the final three guidelines to finalize the end-to-end flow, this is exactly what they can do.

To achieve Operational Excellence in the office, it is important to proceed through the guidelines step by step, in order, and not skip any of them.

Overlooking any individual guideline will omit a critical piece of the design for flow and leave a deficiency that is impossible to make up or accommodate for elsewhere. This is a good point to emphasize when teaching the design guidelines, as missing or deliberately skipping any one of them will typically allow someone to make decisions on what to work on next, which would interrupt the design of how flow should work every day.

9

The Tour

As we walked through the hallways to the industrial claims processing area, I had an unexpected feeling of excitement, like a kid at a birthday party about to unwrap the big gift. Jennifer had presented a really good case for Operational Excellence. She explained the need for flow, how to create it, and even discussed ways to identify broken flow and empower the team to repair it. It all made sense, and now I was looking forward to seeing it in action.

Just before we set foot in the office, Jennifer stopped us and said, "Let me give you a quick overview of what you'll see on the tour. Generally speaking, we're going to follow the flow from when a claim is initiated all the way through to the last step before it goes out to the customer. First, we're going to visit the area where flow begins for industrial claims processing. After that, we'll see a claims preparation cell, which prepares work for the claims processing cell, the last place we'll visit. Any questions? All right, then; let's get to it."

We made our way to the first area. When we arrived, I stood back and took it in. There were two rows of cubicles separated by a center hallway. The row on the left was marked by a sign that said "Information Reconciliation—All Claims," and the row on the right was identified by a sign that said "Industrial Claims Initialization Point." I saw what looked like a first in, first out or FIFO lane feeding the row of cubicles on the right. It seemed like these two areas were connected, but I was not sure exactly how, so I turned to Jennifer.

"Does the reconciliation area feed its work to the claims area through that FIFO rack?" I asked.

"I'm glad you can see that," she replied. "The reconciliation area handles all the incoming traffic for our industrial claims processing division as well as a substantial amount of volume for other areas, which means it's one of our major shared resources."

"OK, but why don't the industrial claims people reconcile their own claims?" I asked.

"Good question," she said. "As I'm sure is the case with your business, when claims reach us, they're liable to be missing all sorts of information. To obtain that data, we may need to contact several people from different departments or even doctors, hospitals, patients, and other outside entities.

"So, instead of randomly chasing the missing information, we set up workflow cycles and bring people together at preset times every day to acquire it. Any requests for information or clarification take place right here, whether the source is internal or external. The associates reconcile claims while they're together and then feed them to the appropriate areas through FIFO. Remember, we don't want to release claims with missing information into the flow because they'll disrupt it."

"So, you've essentially taken all the chaos that used to exist everywhere in the office and front-loaded it to this area," I said.

"In a way, yes," Jennifer replied. "We moved all of the variation that disrupted flow to the front where we can see it and address it. However, we also think of this area as one of the key points where we capture knowledge. Remember, in the office, we flow information and capture knowledge. Because we need to have certain knowledge to process the claim in flow, we make sure we have it before we release the claim. We can also use this knowledge as a reference point for future claims that present us with similar challenges. That way, we won't have to try to solve the same problem twice, or even more often, like we used to."

"That's pretty interesting," responded Peyton, as I nodded in agreement.

"And, what about the row of cubicles?" I asked. "What happens when claims enter the FIFO rack?"

Jennifer pointed to the cubicles on her right and said, "Once claims have all the information they need, the employees follow standard work to determine the order in which they are placed into the FIFO lane that feeds this area. This is the initialization point for industrial claims, the exact point at which claims are released into the flow for industrial claims processing.

"When an associate finishes the claim he or she is working on, the associate simply withdraws the claim that's next in line in the FIFO lane. It's first come, first served—no shuffling priorities, no changing the sequence.

It's already been set using standard work based on what's best for the business. Once the claim hits the FIFO lane, it remains in that sequence all the way to the customer."

"So, once a claim is pulled from the FIFO rack and released into the flow, there are no outstanding issues with it, right?" I asked.

"That's right, Pat," said Jennifer. "Since the associates in the cubicles on the right have all the information they need, they should be able to do their work without any issues. And, because of the workflow cycles that govern this area, once a claim gets here, it's guaranteed to leave within 3 hours. From there, the flow continues, and the rest of the workflow cycles kick in. Because of those workflow cycles, we know that at this point in the flow, each claim is precisely 5 days away from the customer. In fact, we're so confident in that time frame, we even post it."

Jennifer pointed to a sign that was fixed to the side of one of the cubicles (Figure 9.1). I had to admit, the sign was impressive. I gathered my thoughts about everything I'd seen and said, "It sounds like the biggest pain point for this area is that incoming claims still don't have complete information. If you could move them through the information reconciliation area faster, you'd be able to get them out to the customer sooner."

"That's right," said Jennifer. "That's one of the things we're going to address next. We'll be working with our customers to develop flow-level standard work between us and them, which we expect will eliminate a lot of the chaos. Then, our next step is to teach our customers, doctor's offices, hospitals, and so on the techniques they need to create guaranteed turnaround times for responding to our inquiries. Once we have more experience under our belt, we'd love to teach them about Operational Excellence in its entirety. Any questions about the initialization point?"

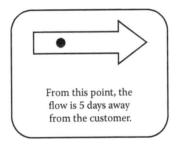

From this point, the
flow is 5 days away
from the customer.

FIGURE 9.1
A sign indicating that the GTT for the flow is 5 days once work reaches this point.

"It all seems to make sense, but it's a lot to take in," I said.

Peyton nodded, and Jennifer said, "Let's continue and follow the flow to the next area, which is our claims preparation cell. This cell combines information from the customer, account managers, and adjusters and prepares it for the claims processing cell, which we will see after this. Everyone at the claims preparation cell will be busy, but we can pull some people away briefly to answer any questions you might have."

We made our way back through the corridors and headed toward a group of four people arranged around a set of tables. Before we got there, Peyton noticed something on the wall and stopped. I saw it, too, and said to Jennifer, "That looks like what you drew on the flip chart back in the conference room."

I recognized the workflow cycle symbol, and the information below it identified this group of people as the claims preparation cell. It also said they flowed work every day for 4 hours, beginning at 1 p.m., and I noticed a sign I had seen at our first stop, but with different information here (Figure 9.2).

"I'm surprised you recognize it, given my lack of artistic talent," said Jennifer.

"Wow," I said. "They're so confident in their workflow cycles that they've posted their guaranteed turnaround times at every point in the flow."

"Well, it's true we post them, but it's not because of confidence," said Jennifer. "We want everyone to know not only how the information flows, but also the timing of the flow. Our goal is to make it so apparent that even a visitor can tell. So, what do you think? Are we successful?"

"Sure, I can follow it," answered Peyton. "It's quite easy. How about you, Pat?"

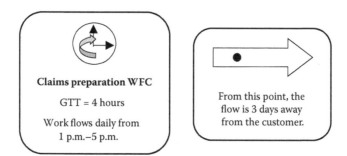

FIGURE 9.2

A sign indicating the name, timing, and GTT of the Claims Preparation Cell and another sign indicating that the GTT for the flow is 3 days once work reaches this point. WFC, workflow cycle.

"Well, I've been in offices before that have lots of signs," I said. "But I've never seen visuals like this that describe the flow. They're intuitive, and I can easily follow them, but I do have a question. I saw a sign at the initialization point that said the flow is 5 days away from the customer. But here, the same sign says the flow is 3 days away. Have I missed something?"

"Not at all, Pat," said Jennifer. "Don't forget that there are different types of workflow cycles. Some are associated with the cells themselves, and others encompass the connections between the cells. Our initialization point connects to the claims preparation cell through a FIFO lane, and the work sits in the FIFO lane for 1 day before the claims preparation cell processes it. That's why the initialization point is 5 days away from the customer and the claims preparation cell is 3, not 4."

"I see," I said. "So, the time associated with a workflow cycle could also encompass the wait time in the FIFO lane plus the time it will take the next area to process the work?"

"That's right," replied Jennifer. "Remember, workflow cycles refer to the rate at which work moves or flows within or between different areas or activities along a specific pathway, and they happen at preset times. A short pathway might be the processing cell itself, while a longer one might be the combination of two processing cells and the FIFO connection between them. We've tried to create ours so the associates in the workflow cycle can see the end-to-end flow within that cycle."

"That makes sense," I said. "It seems like that would help everyone see the flow of value, especially their part in it." I focused my attention on the people in the claims preparation cell and asked Jennifer, "Can I ask some questions?"

"Ask away," said Jennifer. She introduced me to one of the associates, a woman named Wendy, who occupied the first position in the claims preparation cell.

After the introductions, I asked, "So, how can you or anyone here know whether you're on time?"

"Well, we're able to monitor the flow throughout the day by that FIFO lane right there," said Wendy (Figure 9.3). "It's really a whiteboard that we turned into a FIFO lane.

"The circles are whiteboard magnets and represent individual claims. We write the last four digits of a claim number on each magnet, so we always know what to work on next. When we're ready to work on the next job, we remove the right-most magnet from the whiteboard FIFO lane and

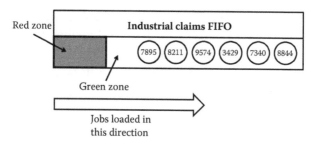

FIGURE 9.3

A whiteboard turned into a color-coded FIFO lane. If work has backed up into the red zone, then the employees know something has gone wrong and abnormal flow exists, and they (not management) can take steps to correct the abnormal flow.

locate that claim. We've even color-coded the FIFO lane green and red to show us if things are going right or wrong. Green is good—everything is going OK. If work is in the red, we have to do something. We're good right now, but if we received two more claims, we'd have abnormal flow, and we'd have to react to it. It's a pretty easy way to know if we're on time just by looking at the flow."

"OK," I said. "But when will your boss or supervisor know if things are on time?"

"Every day at 5 p.m.," answered Wendy. "That's when we normally finish processing everything, and we use pitch to show that, too. If he happens to just walk by, he can tell also by looking at the FIFO board. At the end of the workflow cycle for the claims preparation cell, we put a green flag on top of the tables here. About 5 minutes later, our supervisor comes around. If he sees the green flag, he knows everything got out on time today. It takes about 30 seconds out of his day. It's that quick, and there's an added benefit as well."

"What's that?" I asked.

"The boss hardly bothers us anymore, if you know what I mean," she said.

"But, what if things haven't gotten out on time?" I pressed. "Don't you think he'd want to know before the end of the workflow cycle?"

"True," said Wendy. "The boss can walk by any time and see if work is backed up into the red zone. If it is, he might check in with us to see if we're following the correct standard work to deal with it or if we need any other help. Once in a while, we do, but not too often. Usually, we recognize we're drifting into red territory, and we know how to take care of it ourselves. Even if he sees we're continuing to work past our normal workflow cycle end time because of higher-than-normal customer demand, he knows we're taking care of it."

"Thanks," I said. "That clears things up for me."

"Any time," said Wendy.

I was beginning to see what Operational Excellence looked like. Their supervisor only spends about 30 seconds a day checking to see if things are on time? That is incredible. I was anxious to find out more and recalled the five key questions for flow in the office Jennifer introduced me to earlier in the day. I decided to test them out on one of the people working in the cell. If the questions really were as powerful and meaningful as Jennifer said, then anyone here should be able to answer them. Since Wendy happened to be right next to me, I decided to ask her.

"Wendy, do you mind if I bother you for a few more minutes?" I asked.

"Not at all," she replied. "What else can I do for you?"

"I just have some basic questions I was wondering if you could answer," I said.

"I'll do my best," she said. "Fire away."

"How do you know what to work on next?" I asked.

"That one's easy," said Wendy, pointing to the rack. "I do whatever is next in the FIFO lane right there. I just grab the next magnet, find the corresponding file, and get to it. It's first come, first served."

That also answered my next question, Where do you get your work from?

"All right. How long should it take you to perform your work?" I asked.

"Well, the claims are all a little different, depending on the type," she said. "But, each type has a standard time associated with it, and I can usually process the claim in that amount of time."

I was beginning to understand the power of these five questions. They took care of everything involved with normal flow and eliminated the need for management intervention.

"OK, last two questions," I said. "Where do you send your work once you're finished with it? And when you send your completed work, are you able to tell if flow is still normal?"

"Here I was worried that these questions were going to be difficult," said Wendy. "Jennifer already taught us the five key questions for flow in the office. Once I'm finished with my work, I send it to the next person, who happens to be the account manager in the claims preparation cell. We even mark the exact location with a big circle that says 'Next' on it. The space should always be unoccupied by the time I go to put my file there. If the previous file hasn't been taken from the space yet, then I know something is wrong, so it's easy to tell if the flow is normal or abnormal."

"Thanks again," I said.

Wow, not only did Wendy know the answer to all five questions, but also she obviously understood their purpose. It was impressive to see how ingrained Operational Excellence was in the culture.

Wendy said her good-byes, and Jennifer motioned over someone else from the processing cell so I could talk to him. He introduced himself as Steve, and we distanced ourselves a little bit from the group.

"So, tell me the truth," I asked. "Have the changes really made your life easier?"

"Oh, without a doubt," said Steve. "Everything's much more intuitive now, and we can all see how things are supposed to work. If there's a problem, everyone can see it. Before, we just heard about it afterward from management. If I have any questions, I simply ask my neighbor, who is always there when we prepare a claim. We don't have to chase people for information anymore, so there's a lot less disruption in my day. In fact, I probably deal with half the number of e-mails and voice mails I used to, and we haven't had any fiascoes with our customers in quite a while."

Fiascoes—Mercy Hospital, the catalyst for my visit here, flashed into my mind, and all at once my work problems came rushing back.

"You said life is easier, but what about your customers?" I asked. "Do you think the changes have made them happy as well?"

"I think they might actually be happier than we are," he said. "With the guaranteed turnaround times, we now know how far away a claim is from the customer at every step in the flow. We don't have to guess any more, we *know*, and the lead time has gotten significantly shorter for everyone."

"But, what about when there are problems?" I asked. "How is this process any better than the way things used to be done?"

"Well, problems are going to happen no matter what system you have. We certainly have fewer problems now than in the past, but when they do occur, at least we're able to see them, react to them, and hopefully fix them before they have an impact on the customer, and we don't need management standing over our shoulder all the time. That's a big change from how things were before."

Jennifer came over and said we were ready to move to the last area. On the walk, she reminded us we were going to see the claims processing cell.

We arrived at a conference room, smaller than the one we had been in all morning. It had some tables, computers, and chairs, and between the computer terminals were circles with the word *Next* written in them. I could also see inbound and outbound FIFO lanes, and the inbound one seemed broken up into two sections, one red and the other green. I also saw two signs I was familiar with by now (Figure 9.4).

"This is the claims processing cell," said Jennifer. "Just like at our last cell, remember that we really have two levels of workflow cycles here. One governs the claims processing cell itself, and the other governs the connection between this cell and the claims preparation cell. They're both important because only together do they create a guaranteed turnaround time for the entire flow."

Right at 2 p.m., a group of five people came in, sat down, greeted each other, and began working. Jennifer walked us around to the different associates and introduced us. All of them said that if we had any questions, we should feel free to ask. Rather than jump right in, Jennifer suggested that Peyton and I stand back and watch them work for a little bit.

After observing for about 10 minutes, I saw something remarkable happen. One of the associates in the flow took a folder off a circle that said "Next" on it, opened it up, examined it for a few moments, and then sent it

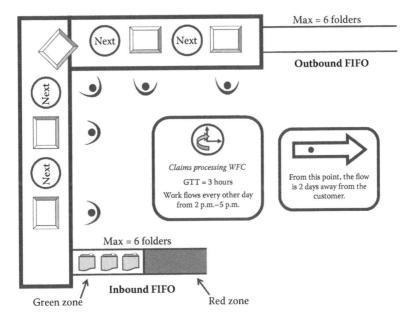

FIGURE 9.4
The layout, timing, GTT, and flow of work for the Claims Processing Cell.

back to the previous associate. I motioned for Jennifer to step outside the conference room so I could ask her a question.

"What just happened there?" I asked. "I saw someone pick up a folder like they were going to start working on it, but instead they just returned it."

"Well, I can't say specifically what happened without going over and asking," said Jennifer. "But, I'm pretty sure the previous associate in the flow did something wrong on the file, so it was sent back."

"Just like that?" I asked. "No one had to check or approve it?"

Jennifer looked slightly puzzled at my question. "No, why would they? Each associate knows what work they should receive, so if something is missing, they just send it back. That's one of the great things about flow. Before, the associate would put the folder on his or her desk and, of course, stop the flow. Then, the voice mails and e-mails would begin."

I remembered what Steve had told me earlier about the number of his voice mails and e-mails being cut in half.

"In the processing cells, the associates are able to see flow beginning to break down and take steps to fix it, *without a meeting and without management intervention*," said Jennifer.

I nodded, and we returned to the claims processing cell. Jennifer noted that everyone always knows what to work on next because they are working in flow that happens along a preset pathway. I asked her if I could ask one of the associates a question, and she said it was not a problem, so I went up to the first associate in the processing cell.

"Excuse me," I said, pointing to the rack of folders that made up the FIFO lane. "I was wondering if you could tell me why your inbound FIFO lane is divided into two sections."

"Sure thing," came the reply. "That's how we're able to tell what the customer demand is for the day. There are two sections to the FIFO lane, red and green. Depending on how many folders we have on a given day, we make adjustments as needed. If only the green section is filled, we don't run the workflow cycle for the full 3 hours."

"Are there any meetings or managers involved in the decision?" I asked.

I got a look that suggested I should have known the answer already. "We haven't done that in a while. We just take care of it ourselves. We like it that way. Besides, my manager's got more important things to do with her time."

I went back to where Jennifer and Peyton were standing, then Jennifer led us out of the conference room, saying thank you to the associates as we left. Once outside, I had one more question.

"How has Operational Excellence affected your ability to hit your promise dates?" I asked Jennifer.

"It's had an extremely positive impact," she replied. "We've not only significantly reduced the overall claims processing time, but we're able to hit the new time consistently because we have workflow cycles and guaranteed turnaround times at the cell and connection level everywhere in our flow. We know this because it's one of the things we measure. After all, in business, you are what you measure.

"Think of it this way. Imagine you were the supervisor or manager in charge of the claims processing cell we just saw. As a leader, if you knew that group flowed information for 3 hours every other day, would you need to chase after them to find out when their work would be finished?"

"Well, it'd be a bit of a mental adjustment to make, but I suppose not," I said. "If this is the way things worked all the time, then I wouldn't need to call people and ask them when they were going to complete their work."

"That's right," said Jennifer. "That's the power of having workflow cycles and guaranteed turnaround times."

OK, I thought, that makes sense. The workflow cycles and guaranteed turnaround times eliminate the need to constantly check on people.

Jennifer turned to both of us and said, "OK, there's one final question I have to ask you both, and it's one that tests how well we've done in this area. Take a quick look back inside the conference room."

We did as she asked and then came back outside. "Can you tell if our flow is on time right now just by looking? Are things normal, or is there a problem?"

Neither one of us was expecting this question. We took one more look at the processing cell, and Peyton was first to respond. "Everything looks fine. I don't see anything in a red zone, so it looks like they're on time."

"I agree," I added. "Work hasn't accumulated past the green zone of the FIFO lane, so it looks good."

"That's right," said Jennifer. "Just remember, the point isn't that everything is going well right now, although that's of course good. The point is that you can *tell* if it is just by looking—no questions, no meetings, no status updates."

She paused for a few moments to let that sink in. "Are you ready to head back to the conference room and wrap up?"

Peyton and I both nodded and followed Jennifer back through the corridors. When we got to our conference room, I had some questions about the tour, so we all sat down.

"Everything looked very impressive, and I'm not only talking about the flow, but also the associates' attitudes," I said. "They were proud of the changes. In my office, well—people like doing things their own way. If you try to change anything, it just leads to meeting after meeting. How did you get the associates not only to do things differently but also to *enjoy* doing things differently?"

Jennifer let out a deep breath. "That's an excellent point," she said. "The physical changes to the office are one thing, but changing people is something else entirely. I'll admit it was difficult. There's a whole other chapter in change management that we didn't talk about today.

"When we began implementing the new concepts, we encountered people who had been employed with the company for years, and they were very knowledgeable. Each person had their own method for getting things done, and I'm not just talking about the associates. I'm talking about their managers, too. At first, the managers didn't want people leaving their areas to join processing cells or workflow cycles. They wanted them to be available to work on priorities.

"We had to educate everyone on the concepts of Operational Excellence and how we use it to grow the business. Creating awareness and aligning the managers was key. We had to teach everyone that it's not about increasing efficiency. It's about creating a foundation for business growth.

"Most people didn't see why we needed to create flow and establish standard work, but some did, and we worked with those people first. It was easier to persuade everyone else to give it a try once they saw it in action. We gave them some ownership in growing the business, too, and this helped put everyone at ease. After all, everyone wants to see the company grow."

"That makes sense," I said. "It also sounds like quite a bit of work."

"It sure does," added Peyton. "But, then again, they did it here, and it's unlike anything I've ever seen. It's quite an accomplishment. You must be proud."

"We couldn't have done it without the associates," said Jennifer. "They're the real reason for our success. I give them all the credit."

Peyton and I both nodded.

"There's something else from the tour I want to ask you about," I said. "All the work was passed in folders. It was all hard copy, and even the magnets I saw on the whiteboard FIFO lane represented physical work. Everything could be held in your hand. But, in many offices, the work is all electronic. In large companies, people send e-mails back and forth from different buildings and may never be in the same room. What do you do in situations like that?"

"That's a great question," said Jennifer. "We still want to follow the same process and use the same techniques we've been talking about. However, the application will be a little different. Let's just say there are many ways to create end-to-end flow by following the guidelines. The only limit to your specific situation is your creativity. If you can find a way to answer the five key questions for flow in the office, you should be OK.

"For example, we can create rules for our e-mail inboxes so messages are sent into electronic FIFO lanes via different preestablished subfolders. From there, we'd process each subfolder on a workflow cycle, the same way we process work in the FIFO racks and boards you saw on the tour. Off-site locations would establish their own workflow cycles to flow information to each subfolder by the time it's needed."

"I can see how the guidelines could simplify the flow between different branches all over the country," said Peyton.

"That's exactly what they've done for us," said Jennifer, pausing before continuing. "Great discussion. Your questions have reminded me just how much we've accomplished. Before we conclude, I want to thank both of you for taking time out of your day to come here and visit with us. I hope you learned a lot of practical knowledge so far, but we've got one more critical topic to cover, so I'd like to wrap up with a final thought. I'd like for you to think of what it is you *didn't* see while we were out on the tour."

Peyton and I both looked at each other for a second, then thought about it. What did we not see? There could be a million different answers to that question, but I sensed Jennifer was after something specific. I thought back to the conversation we had just had about workflow cycles and guaranteed turnaround times and how Peyton and I knew the claims processing cell was on time just by looking, and then it hit me.

"Managers," I said. "We didn't see any managers or supervisors on the tour. No one was walking around checking on things or putting out fires. We also didn't see any hot lists, expedites, or changing priorities. There weren't any meetings taking place in any of the open rooms either. Does management even have meetings to set priorities anymore?"

"Not really," replied Jennifer. "We had a few when we first implemented the system, but we've virtually eliminated them. Which leads me to my final point of the day: Remember one of the things we said earlier about Operational Excellence? It's a foundation for business growth. Our objective is to grow the business. This is why Operational Excellence is the destination of the continuous improvement journey. A seamless, smooth-running operation *enables managers to spend their time working on offense.*"

Offense? I thought. Are we talking about football?

"Working on offense means performing activities that grow the business as opposed to maintaining or defending it," said Jennifer. "Think about it. If you're out there chasing claims, people, and resources all day, how will you ever have the time you need to grow your business? To grow your business, you need *time*. And our managers and supervisors now have *time* to work on offense.

"This is why we work so hard following and implementing the business process guidelines for flow. We do it for one reason: to give our people the time they need to grow the business."

It all made sense to me now. The business process guidelines for flow were enough of a paradigm shift. To find out they were also a means to an even greater end—that was incredible. For years, I had just been trying to improve my office for efficiency and productivity, when I really should have been trying to improve it to *grow the business*.

I stood up to leave and went over and shook Jennifer's hand, then Peyton's.

"Thanks for everything," I said. "Now, I've got to go back and convince my boss that I haven't been dreaming all day."

Jennifer chuckled a little before saying, "Don't worry. It won't be as hard as it seems. Just remember everything we talked about today, especially how Operational Excellence creates a foundation for business growth and frees up management to work on offense. If your boss is anything like mine, that'll get eaten up."

I thanked my companions once again and made my way out of the building and to my car. On the drive home and later that night, I could not stop thinking about what I had learned and seen.

How could I possibly explain it all to Chris tomorrow?

FROM THE AUTHOR

One of the more challenging aspects of making flow visual is doing so with work that is primarily digital in nature. When the majority of work is performed and then transmitted via e-mail or "lives" in networked databases, work can too easily remain hidden from view, and making flow visual is a critical component of Operational Excellence. Without visual flow, it is difficult to distinguish between normal and abnormal flow in the day-to-day workings of the office.

While every effort should be made to make the digital work physical when practical to do so, sometimes the best we can do is *represent* digital work in some physical way. For example, a system of visual signals like flags can be used to indicate whether a processing cell has completed its work on time. In this case, the work itself has not been made physical, but insight into whether its completion is on time or behind has been created in a way that physically can be seen in the office.

A more dynamic workflow might involve a different solution to make the flow visual, perhaps by representing each piece of digital work in an engineering department via color-coded tokens on a magnetic whiteboard. The board can be divided into FIFO lanes per type of work. As the electronic work is processed through the designed flow first in, first out, the tokens are correspondingly moved on the whiteboard first in, first out. This enables everyone to physically see if the flow is on time or behind just by looking at the whiteboard, which acts as a window into the status of the digital work. The tokens could be moved at the end of every workflow cycle if it is not practical to move them in real time as the digital work is completed, as this would still provide insight into the timeliness of the overall flow by knowing if the workflow cycles had been completed according to the established guaranteed turnaround time.

Creating visual flow is key to preventing management intervention over the long term. Remember—your visuals for flow should be so good that even a visitor can tell if you are on time. Visual flow enables leadership to understand the status and timeliness of work on a day-to-day basis without asking questions. If there *is* a need to ask questions, then they can be focused on the system of flow, such as the following:

- Are the workflow cycles on time?
- Is the correct takt capability being used?
- Are we following the correct standard work for abnormal flow?

These questions focus on the system of flow, what (if anything) has gone wrong with it, and most important, what can be done *within the rules of flow* to fix something if it has gone wrong. It is vital that management responses stay within the boundaries of the system of flow created. Otherwise, the impression becomes that the designed flow is really only useful part of the time. Soon enough, however, "part of the time" begins to happen more and more frequently until the office is eventually dependent on management to get work to the customer again.

To this end, educating management is as important as educating the employees themselves. While there are many aspects of Operational Excellence and flow design that management should learn, among the most important teaching points is what questions managers should ask their teams. The questions should center on the key concepts of flow and Operational Excellence, but the common thread between them is that the managers should know the answers before the questions are asked. The intent is to confirm that the employees have the knowledge about flow and Operational Excellence that they should. If employees can answer questions about the end-to-end flow correctly, then it means they also have a solid understanding of its individual components and how they relate to one another.

Checking the employees' understanding like this also provides a way for management to show active support for the transformation to Operational Excellence. This support assists in driving cultural change throughout the organization by sending the message that Operational Excellence is simply the way things are done, not just a passing trend, and this can help build momentum during the implementation once everyone sees that management is not only on board but also fully vested in its success.

10

Sharing the Knowledge

When the alarm sounded on Friday, I bolted out of bed, anxious to get to the office to meet with Chris. What a week! Only four mornings ago, I learned about the mess that had happened while I was away, but what I've seen and heard since then has changed the way I look at the office. I was aware of the tough sell ahead and the skepticism I expected to encounter, but I was also ready for the challenge.

I got into my car and headed to work, rehearsing the pending encounter with Chris along the way. I parked and, as I walked to the office, noticed Chris looking at me from the window on the third floor, as if awaiting my arrival. At that moment, I was glad I had prepared for this discussion.

The ride up the elevator seemed to take forever. As the doors opened, Chris met me, seemingly eager to hear about my field trip the previous day, and we walked straight into my office. I did not even have a chance to check my e-mail.

"I'm really interested in what you learned from the benchmarking trip," said Chris. "Mercy Hospital called again and wants an update on how we are going to correct things. It sure would be good to have a plan to share with them before this escalates."

I took a deep breath and gathered my thoughts.

"OK," I said. "As we're both aware, we discovered a downward trend in our performance that we need to correct or we risk alienating or losing Mercy Hospital and other major customers. Because some of our smaller customers have tremendous potential for growth, any plan we put in place has to take care of all of our customers, not just the ones who are most important right now. I won't bother going into any more detail on these issues since you're as familiar with them as I am."

"Possibly more familiar," said Chris. "But who's keeping score, right?"

"Right," I said.

Well, no point in wasting any time. "Let me get right into what I saw and heard yesterday, what my approach was when I first got there, and what I'd like to share with you today. For starters, I admit that I was hoping I'd be able to simply copy what they did there and use it here to solve our problems. We've been using some continuous improvement tools ever since I got here, so I figured if this other company was using them better or more effectively, I'd just see how they did it and try to do the same thing here.

"But they looked at continuous improvement differently. They had moved beyond solving problems, eliminating waste, and simply trying to get better each day. They looked at creating Operational Excellence. They set a destination for what they were trying to accomplish with their continuous improvement efforts, and because they knew where they were going, they were able to get there much faster."

"That's interesting," said Chris. "You mentioned Operational Excellence. Every company says that's what they're striving for, even us. Aren't we doing that already?"

"Not exactly," I said. "We're just trying to continuously improve by using the latest tools, but they're trying to get to a place where *each and every employee can see the flow of value to the customer and fix that flow before it breaks down.* That's how they define Operational Excellence, and it's by far the most practical and applicable definition I've ever heard."

"Hmmm," said Chris, letting that sink in. "That's quite a definition, and when I think about it, that's pretty much exactly what I want to see happening here. I like it. Keep going."

"Well, I went there looking to solve our problems, but now, I'm seeing things from a much broader perspective. It's not about looking for solutions to problems. It's about *growing our business.*"

"Growing our business?" repeated Chris. "I'm starting to like this even more."

"It was quite an insight," I said. "We strive for Operational Excellence not only to create self-healing flow but also to grow our business."

"Sounds good," said Chris. "But how do we do that when we're still having problems with some of our key customers?"

"This is the real beauty of it," I said. "We're going to do it by *following a process.* One of the first things I learned yesterday was that we can't just copy their solution and use it here, but we can copy the *process* they used."

"OK, that makes sense," said Chris. "Our business is different from theirs anyway."

"Even better, *a process can be taught*," I said. "It can be shared with everyone in the company and used again and again to generate results. This is how they changed over there, and it's how we can change here, too."

"It must be some process," said Chris, with a little disbelief. "But, I like what you said about how we're able to teach it to everyone. That's a good thought. Tell me more."

I felt like I was getting somewhere.

"Sure thing," I said. "One of the first things I learned was that we want to create flow through our office. To determine if we have flow, we need to ask five questions, and if we can answer them all successfully, we have flow. I won't get into the details of those questions now, but suffice it to say that everything is so systematic that even something as seemingly simple as creating flow is done by following a process."

"OK, so there's a process for creating flow," said Chris. "That's supposed to transform this office into something spectacular?"

"Not by itself," I said. "The five questions I just mentioned are used to determine whether we have flow. There's actually a nine-step process to create flow through the entire office, one that we can teach and everyone can learn. It includes things like processing cells; workflow cycles; standard work at the activity and flow levels; and pitch to tell us whether we're on time. And, get this: If we have flow through our entire office, then we can establish a guaranteed turnaround time for every single claim we receive.

"One of the things I learned is that we should flow information along predetermined, physical pathways at preset times and in first in, first out or FIFO fashion. Everyone knows the pathways and timing involved, so they know when they'll get the information they need. No one has to make any phone calls or chase people or information. Once that flow is established, we make it so everyone can tell normal flow from abnormal flow just by looking. The result is that the flow self-heals when things start to go wrong. The associates fix the flow before it breaks down, and they do so *without management intervention*."

"This is a breakthrough," said Chris. "It's a different way of thinking, and it sounds like just what we need. But, you talked about growing our business. How is this process going to do that?"

"By freeing up management to work on *offense*," I said, surprised at how fluidly that rolled off my tongue. "By offense, I mean growing the business. We use a nine-step process to create flow through our entire office, but again, the secret is that the associates handle it all by themselves. They're able to see when it's about to break down and fix it on their own. Once the system is in place, there's practically no management intervention whatsoever. Because managers aren't spending their time chasing claims, people, and resources, they finally have the time they need to grow the business."

Chris leaned back and let out a deep breath before speaking. "You know, I've been trying to figure out how to explain that to people for a long time now. I'm getting pressure from the top to spend more of my time generating new business, but I don't *have* the time because I'm here 10 hours a day as it is just making sure everything gets done.

"I like it, Pat. I have to tell you, you've killed two *big* birds with one stone. Putting in self-healing flow that creates guaranteed turnaround times *and* frees up management to work on offense? I can see our market share growing already. So, I have two questions for you. How long, and how much?"

"That's what's so great about Operational Excellence," I said. "It takes months, not years, because everyone works toward a common destination and follows the same process to get there. As for the cost, it's all education, and whatever expense we incur will no doubt be offset by the business we gain and fiascoes we avoid. No more Mercy Hospital breathing down our necks, no more shuffling priorities, no more wondering when a claim will be completed."

"So you, we, our company, can do all of this right now?" asked Chris.

"Well, I understand the concepts and think I can give them a shot," I said. "After what I saw yesterday, I know there's a lot more to learn. The first thing we need to do is get the executives aligned and onboard. That's one of the most important steps. Without understanding at the top of the organization, everything else becomes a lot more complicated. Then, we use education to get everyone—executives, managers, and associates— moving toward a common destination of Operational Excellence."

I paused to catch my breath, eyeing Chris and looking for a reaction. "So, what do you think?" I asked.

"I think I need to get educated. Put me first on the list. And Pat—good job."

FROM THE AUTHOR

The culmination of a transformation to Operational Excellence is working on *offense*, or activities that grow the business. In fact, many companies, as they begin their implementation of Operational Excellence, start tracking how much time they spend working on offense and the frequency with which management intervenes in the flow. Often, the amount of time spent working on offense is somewhat low and the frequency of management intervention is rather high.

As the implementation gets under way and nears completion, however, and if the guidelines have been followed and applied correctly to create self-healing flow, the amount of time spent working on offense should increase dramatically as managers are no longer required to spend significant portions of their day fixing problems with the flow. This freed-up time is now spent exclusively working on the activities that grow the business and typically increases significantly once self-healing flow has been fully implemented.

The reduction in management intervention and ability of leadership to work on offense are the primary channels through which the nine guidelines are linked to business growth. Applying the guidelines creates self-healing, autonomous flow in the office, and this is what frees management's time to work on offense because the employees are now able to fix problems with the flow on their own.

But, it is not only management's time that is freed to work on offense once the office has implemented self-healing flow and achieved Operational Excellence. *Every* employee will be working on offense, and the type of offense will vary depending on the employee. Senior leadership might spend time meeting with current and potential customers or devising new sales strategies. Frontline employees, on the other hand, might work on enhancing the standard work used to resolve abnormal flow conditions or creating more standard work to handle other abnormal flow conditions not yet encountered. Working on these activities not only enables more flow problems to be fixed quicker but also acts as a barrier that prevents the occurrence of management intervention on an ongoing basis, thereby enabling management to continue working on offense day to day.

In this way, achieving Operational Excellence in the office refocuses the activities of every employee toward offense. While strong results like decreased lead times and faster responses to customers will be realized in an office that has applied the nine guidelines, the true power of Operational Excellence is fulfilled when self-healing flow allows each employee to work on offense and help grow the business.

Applying the nine guidelines, creating self-healing, autonomous flow, and achieving Operational Excellence lays a foundation for sustainable business growth that can be achieved in *months*, not years, and provides a model that can be used perpetually to stay one step ahead of the competition.

Bibliography

Duggan, Kevin J. *Design for Operational Excellence: A Breakthrough Strategy for Business Growth*. New York: McGraw-Hill, 2011.

Duggan, Kevin J. *Creating Mixed Model Value Streams: Practical Lean Techniques for Building to Demand*. 2nd ed. New York: Taylor & Francis, 2013.

Duggan, Kevin J., and Tim Healey. *Operational Excellence in Your Office: A Guide to Achieving Autonomous Value Stream Flow with Lean Techniques*. New York: Taylor & Francis, 2015.

Kennedy, Michael N. *Product Development for the Lean Enterprise*. Richmond, VA: Oklea Press, 2003.

Liker, Jeffery K. *The Toyota Way: 14 Management Principles from the World's Greatest Manufacturer*. New York: McGraw-Hill, 2004.

Rother, Mike, and John Shook. *Learning to See: Value-Stream Mapping to Create Value and Eliminate Muda*. Cambridge, MA: Lean Enterprise Institute, 2003.

Womack, James P., and Daniel T. Jones. *Lean Thinking: Banish Waste and Create Wealth in Your Corporation*. New York: Simon & Schuster, 1996.

Index

Page numbers in italics refer to figures.